T0285404

UnLeadership

UnLeadership

Make Building Relationships Your Business

A Guide for Thoughtful Leaders Like You.

Scott and Alison Stratten

WILEY

Published by John Wiley & Sons, Inc., Hoboken, New Jersey.
Published simultaneously in Canada.

For general information on our other products and services or for technical support, please contact our Customer Care Department within the United States at (800) 762-2974, outside the United States at (317) 572-3993 or fax (317) 572-4002.

Wiley also publishes its books in a variety of electronic formats. Some content that appears in print may not be available in electronic formats. For more information about Wiley products, visit our web site at www.wiley.com.

Library of Congress Cataloging-in-Publication Data is Available:

ISBN: 9781394223381 (cloth)
ISBN: 9781394223398 (ePub)
ISBN: 9781394223404 (ePDF)

Cover design: Paul McCarthy

SKY10064241_010924

To those who do the work, pave the way, connect, nourish, welcome, and inspire.

Thank you.

Contents

1

Leadership in the Age of Disruption

GOOD LEADERSHIP HAS NEVER BEEN more important, but for too long we have imagined leaders as visionaries and risk takers—those out front, with their backs turned. We think about leadership as being "ahead of the game," but we can't effectively lead others without connection and awareness. When we turn our backs to the audience, employees, or fans behind us, we lose the opportunity to truly improve not only ourselves but our products, content, and companies. For the past 15 years, we've written about business in the age of disruption, sharing stories and best practices, what to do and what not to do, in marketing, sales, and branding. Our answer has always been relationships, that if you believe business is built on relationships, you need to make building them your business. The lightning speed of technological innovation, the proliferation and evolution of social media, and a global pandemic have impacted everything, every person, every company, every industry. Everything has changed and nothing is different—people still buy from those they like, know, and trust. In business, relationships matter more than ever. Adding the prefix UN to leadership means putting relationships at the heart of your leadership. You can't effectively

1

lead others without connection; in fact, without relationships, you aren't leading at all.

None of you need a fancy study to know that the majority of people are not thriving and engaged at work (See fancy study: Gallup 2023). Employee stress is at a record high. Even when we are physically present or virtually connected, disengagement (or quiet quitting as the ~~kids~~ old folks say) is leaving our teams unmotivated. One in 10 workers consider their workplace toxic, and even companies with relatively healthy cultures can have pockets of toxicity within teams. The pandemic revealed disparities, and today many managers and executives have the flexibility to continue work remotely, as they call employees back to the office. Employees are fighting back, giving less, and looking for work someplace else. At the same time, there has been an increase in available jobs, meaning employers have to work harder to retain talented employees. With disruption becoming the norm, leaders need to be agile, able to move, connect, and motivate in an increasingly fluid work environment.

Adding the prefix UN to marketing, sales, and branding was also about thinking beyond silos, and leadership is no different. Regardless of title or position, leadership can happen from anywhere. UnLeaders recognize that no company's success is a one-person job. It is about motivation, both the kind that keeps us on our paths and the kind we give to others, our teams, companies, and communities. Leadership is a verb, not a title; it is embodied in our decisions and our relationships. It is a balance between confidently communicating your vision and remaining open to transformation. It's sturdy and nimble, dependable, and flexible. It's navigating uncertainty guided by values, knowing when to hang on and when to let go. Leadership requires connection and awareness because without them, you have no idea what it's like to work for you.

2

What Is UnLeadership?

WHEN YOU THINK ABOUT LEADERSHIP, what do you imagine?

Confidence, charisma maybe, authority perhaps, or account-ability. The person with the biggest platform. Your favorite artist or creator. Your grandparents. Your boss. Your high school art teacher. Yourself. Leaders take ideas and create action. They look over the horizon and guide practice. They see gaps and often make tough choices—those that run counter to a "what we've always done" mentality. Leaders are motivators. They make rough waters feel smooth. Leaders lead with their actions, not just their words. They take responsibility. Leaders are brave and bold but sometimes also the quietest people in the room.

When we set out to write UnLeadership, this is where we started, and for every person we've asked, our definition of leader-ship has only grown; there are many kinds of leaders and many ways to lead. None of us achieves anything alone. There's luck, timing, and hard work of course, but there are also leaders and relationships that teach, guide, open doors, and break barriers. This book includes leadership lessons we've learned along the way, but it is also so much more. Inside is a collection of stories about leadership and what it means to be a leader from people across industries including finance,

3

entertainment, tourism, and education in both for-profit and non-profit spaces and those who have built and led teams, companies, and communities and taken their vision from idea through implementation. We spoke to entrepreneurs and executives, founders, and advocates, many of whom are well established and some just getting started. They've created movements, inspired followers and fandoms, and led companies through transformation and change.

In a series of interviews, we asked what leadership means to them and the lessons they've learned along the way. We spoke about their leadership journey and the lessons and people who've inspired them. We set out to learn their stories and maybe get a few quotations about leadership within their industries—but we ended up with something more. After listening to the interviews, reviewing the transcripts, what revealed itself was a collection of narratives on what it means to be a leader. These stories serve as the antithesis of a "Top five ways anyone can be a better leader," revealing lessons with nuance, complexity, beauty, and inspiration.

We can be pretty cynical around here; that happens when you build a brand off snark. But the truth is, leaders are those who inspire—and we've been inspired. Leaders teach, and we have learned. Leaders make impossible things feel possible—and this book would not be possible without them. We hope their stories will be a compass, that you'll find reflections of your own experiences and lessons you can use today to become a more impactful leader in your company, industry, or community. We believe that business is personal, and we're excited you're here. Taking time to read a book is no small thing, so thank you. Whether you are an entrepreneur, executive, or an aspiring leader with a big idea, we hope you'll find something that speaks to you, informs you, challenges you and travels along with you in your leadership. There is no wrong way to read the stories in this book - skip around, see what resonates, skip as many as you like, and (we hope) read others until the pages are worn. We hope these stories challenge you to see leadership in a new way and that you find lessons to help you grow as a leader.

3

Leadership Is a Creative Profession

In my presentations, I use art as a catalyst—a universal way for an audience to experience art being created, together. It isn't really about the art; it's about the emotional experience when art happens. We tap into the emotional side of the audience, who are oftentimes caught off guard. When you realize that you're sharing an emotional experience with the person next to you, you feel connected on a human level. Through art, the audience becomes an engaged participant. I want to shift the notion of art as a noun, something that hangs dormant on your wall, into an active verb, a process. Similarly with leadership, we must take the notion of leadership as a title and turn it into a verb that is dynamic and adaptable. The definition of a leader will continue to evolve over time—it's on us to be mentally curious and agile.

We often mentor students in their painting and use what we call the contemplation room. It's a space where you can sit and look at your art and wait. It isn't about the finished product; you can go back and change it. Art is never finished, music is never finished, and neither is the process of growing and learning. Leading is a creative profession; it's not a delivery system or automation channel. Leadership is a way to provoke, encourage, and affirm the people around us, to create a bigger picture, a painted picture of the future. The question is, How do we keep our employees and communities aligned to that greater, painted picture—the vision of what we're all trying to accomplish?

—**Erik Wahl,** internationally recognized artist, inspirational speaker, and bestselling author of *Unthink: Rediscover Your Creative Genius*, from our interview, recorded May 30, 2023.

4

UnLeadership Begins with Awareness

AWARENESS IS CRITICAL FOR A leader. Whether you recognize it or not, you bring your emotions and past experiences into work every day. Awareness moves leadership beyond a title and makes it a verb. It begins with self-awareness, understanding that as the boss, you have no idea what it's like to work for you, and recognizing you don't have all the answers and that your position may or may not affect communication and therefore understanding. Beyond even their team or company, UnLeaders focus outside their line of sight; they work toward industry awareness. They see gaps, are curious, and feed that curiosity. They ask questions: Why? How? And most importantly, Why not? They create resources, share their knowledge, and create an easier path for future leaders coming up. Awareness moves leadership beyond title and makes it creative process rather than something you arrive at.

Gerald Ratner inherited a chain of jewelry stores and in less than a decade, turned them into a billion-dollar enterprise. He flipped the industry script, turning away from elitist marketing and focusing on working-class customers, and it worked. Ratner disrupted the industry and became well known as a democratizer—and a very

7

successful one at that. His strategy grew the company from 120 to more than 2000 locations, capturing 50% of the jewelry market in the UK. Ratner's success seemed unstoppable, until April 1991, when he gave a speech that destroyed his business. Advised to put in a few jokes (enter social media manager anxiety here. . .), Ratner called his products "total crap," and insulted the very customers he should have been thanking for his success. "Ratner doesn't represent prosperity—and come to think of it, it has very little to do with quality as well. We do cut-glass sherry decanters complete with six glasses on a silver-plated tray that your butler can serve you drinks on, all for £4.95. People say, 'How can you sell this for such a low price?' I say, because it's total crap." Awareness brought Ratner success, and a lack of awareness took it away. Within a few days, his company shares were down 80%. Awareness is something you have to work at. It cannot end after one success or another. Rather, leaders work to actively maintain connection and keep their ears to the ground.

The importance of awareness to leadership isn't some new concept; in a 1998 study of 200 leading companies, psychologist and best-selling author of *Emotional Intelligence* Daniel Goleman found that effective leadership is distinguished by emotional intelligence (Goleman 1998). Without it, a person can have training, curiosity, and endless ideas, but they won't be a great leader. His research found direct ties between self-awareness, empathy, and motivation that links emotional intelligence with measurable business results. "Every businessperson knows a story about a highly intelligent, highly skilled executive who was promoted into a leadership position only to fail at the job. And they also know a story about someone with solid—but not extraordinary—intellectual abilities and technical skills who was promoted into a similar position and then soared. Such anecdotes support the widespread belief that identifying individuals with the "right stuff" to be leaders is more art than science. After all, the personal styles of superb leaders vary: Some leaders are subdued and analytical; others shout their manifestos from the mountaintops. And just as important, different situations call for different types of leadership. Most mergers need a sensitive negotiator at the helm, whereas many turnarounds require a more forceful authority. I have found, however, that the most effective leaders are alike in one crucial way: they all have a high degree of what has come to be known as emotional intelligence. It's not that IQ and technical skills are irrelevant. They do matter but mainly as "threshold capabilities"; that is, they are the entry-level requirements for executive positions. But my research, along with other recent studies, clearly shows that emotional intelligence is the sine qua non of leadership. Without it, a person can have the best training in the world, an incisive, analytical mind, and an endless supply of smart ideas, but they still won't make a great leader" (Goleman 1998).

Self-awareness also allows us to understand our own leadership style and then how that might impact those we work with; it is the difference between confidence and arrogance. If leadership is our goal, we have to be able to communicate and create structures that call in other people. We've seen a lack of awareness from leadership displayed in some pretty wild ways over the years, like terrifying team building exercises, planned with absolutely no feedback from employees. (No, I would not like to be immersed in a tank of water or touch a tarantula, thank you very much.) Even if you aren't literally risking their lives, what classifies as team building often involves alcohol, athletics, or other social activities, sometimes outside working hours. While we love team building done right, for a leader, it's pretty unlikely the challenges facing your team can be solved by pickleball. The first step to team building is getting to know your team, their challenges, and their strengths. To embody leadership, we have to have organizational awareness, awareness of the needs and wants of those we seek to lead.

5

What is the Archetype of a Leader?

Jonathan Fields, *the* Good Life Guy, *makes things that move people, delivering insights that spark purpose, possibility, and potential. On a decades-long quest to discover what makes people come fully alive, Jonathan is an award-winning author, Webby-nominated producer, business innovator, and host of one of the world's top podcasts,* Good Life Project. *His newest company,* Spark Endeavors, *is built around intellectual property that helps people explore the intersection between meaning and work.*
(Highlights from our interview, recorded May 31, 2023.)

IN MY EARLY YEARS I built anything and everything, from bicycles to houses. In high school and college, I started building businesses, and from there, it's been a series of companies, books, brands, experiences—anything where I can step into a creative process, preferably a co-creative process. It's more fun when we can build with other people, make things that go out into the world, make a difference, and make a ripple in the fabric of the human condition. I work with my wife, Stephanie. We run both companies together. She's an amazing human being and an incredible partner in life and in business. We're very complementary in what we do. I focus more on the big vision, the impact and narrative, and product development. She's an astonishingly gifted experience designer who loves to craft magical moments and interactions that let people feel safe, seen, and celebrated. And, Stephanie is the empathetic and organizational heartbeat that holds our day-to-day operations and teams together.

Most of our team have been together at the Good Life Project for years. They do the work that makes things go into the world and affect millions of people, which is pretty cool. I'm an introvert, a more sensitive human being. Making things that move people allows me to do what I want and creates a healthy buffer for me to have the solitude and the peace that keeps me feeling nourished and comfortable. A big part of why our team has been rolling together for so long is because we model the behavior we want our team to exhibit and invest in their growth, professionally and as human beings. We want everyone we work with to evolve as a person. If you realize this is no longer what you want to be doing, that's okay. I would rather have that happen, bless you on, and find the person where the work makes sense. We look first and foremost at everyone as people, not as cogs in a machine or productivity units. At the end of the day, it's a huge competitive advantage to treat people like human beings.

In leadership, there is an interesting dance between vulnerability and boundaries. All the research shows, if you want to build genuine connected relationships, you have to have mutual progressive vulnerability. That means it has to be two-sided. It has to slowly invite people deeper into it, and it has to be open. You actually have to share things about yourself that you may be uncomfortable with, be open, authentic, and vulnerable. At the same time, part of the role of a leader is to create psychological safety. There's an interesting dance that happens on the razor's edge of vulnerability and safety because you can step over the line where you're being too vulnerable. You think you're connecting with people because you want them to see you as real, but in fact you're breaking the seal of safety in the relationship. Instead of them being willing to open up and share more, they actually start to pull back. It's important to understand the sensitivities and boundaries of those you lead, what is appropriate, and what feels good not just to you but to them. Vulnerability sometimes becomes manufactured. I think the most powerful vulnerability in leadership is when someone admits they don't know the answer, the next step, or the solution, when you admit you don't know and call on your team to collectively work together to figure things out.

Storytelling is critically important, and as a leader, my role in the story is very meaningful to me. The story is the center of everything; it makes hard things possible, and if you get it wrong, it makes even easy things impossible. You need to invite everybody to step into the story and be the hero. This is especially true in the context of a start-up, which can be a pretty brutalizing experience. You're often pushing aggressively, sometimes for years, to figure things out and build structure, resources, and revenue. The story you tell about why you're doing the work is critically important to inspire people to raise their hand initially and stay when things get tough. I've never built a company where we didn't go through a season, if not multiple seasons, where I was at home, at night, shaking with stress and trying to revisit that story myself. It reminds me why I'm still here and not walking away. I have to show up for my team and remind them of the story, bringing us all back to the touch point. People tap out early when adversity comes if your story is just a business outcome. It isn't enough; there has to be something bigger that allows the people participating to derive a sense of meaning.

We've been producing media at the Good Life Project since 2011. Part of our production ethos has always been to record in person, in our own space. My last in-person conversation was in February 2020, with Macy Gray, and soon after that, New York City shut down. We had to make a big decision—shut down the company or take this moment of disruption and use it as an opportunity. We ran a series of experiments to see whether we could find our way to a new, virtual format. There were tough moments and a ton of reimagining. Thankfully it was "figureoutable," and we fully transitioned over. Now I love recording remotely and do a lot less in-person stuff because many of the assumptions I made were wrong. I've had the chance to speak to childhood heroes who were never coming to New York. I sat down with Peter Frampton, whose album I had on my record player nonstop as a kid. It opened up opportunities that to this day remain incredible. Leadership means being open to change and shifting and reframing your horizon.

Spark Endeavors is based on the idea that we all have within us a set of fundamental impulses to exert effort in a particular way for no other reason than the feeling it gives us, a feeling of meaningfulness, purpose, energy, and excitement and easier access to that blissed-out state of flow of fully expressed identity and potential. We researched and identified 10 different impulses, and around each of these, an identifiable set of behaviors, tendencies, and preferences that form archetypes. We call them Sparketypes®, a fun shorthand to say the archetypes for work that spark you. We developed an assessment that helped people figure out what impulses are strongest in them, motivating them to work hard at something for no other reason than that feeling and the type of work that repels them the most. We launched and came out of beta after about a year in development at the end of 2018. Right now, about 850,000 people have completed it. We're sitting on a massive dataset of 40 million-plus data points with follow-up surveys showing that when people do their Sparketype's® work, they're more likely to feel energized and excited and have a stronger sense of meaning and purpose.

My advice to aspiring leaders is to spend more time developing your insides than your outsides. When we begin riding into management or leadership or start our own thing, we tend to be in a mad rush. We panic—what books can I read, what are the strategies, the processes? What are the tools, the ecosystems, and the spreadsheets? But even if you have all the skills in the world, if you're not self-aware, it won't work. You have to devote an equal, if not greater, amount of time to getting to know yourself and becoming self-aware. Focus inward, and understand who you are and what matters to you.

Then build the skill, craft, process, and strategy around that. If you don't do that, you show up as a bundle of skills without a heart and a core. People will feel your lack of self-awareness and alignment with essence because you can't align your actions with your essence if you have no idea what your essence is. Sometimes people can't distinguish between what's meaningful and what makes them happy. Although it's awesome to be happy, the thing that sustains people is meaning, especially when things get hard. Who are you? What triggers you? What brings you calm and peace? What are your values? What do you aspire to? What energizes you? What would you work nonstop for, for hours, weeks, months, and years, simply because it meant that much to you and made you feel that good?

6

Heroic Leadership

LAUREN MAILLIAN IS AN AWARD-WINNING marketer, prolific investor, advisor, entrepreneur, author, and board member. She has advised and invested in over 40 start-ups, and her portfolio represents over $5 billion in market capitalization. She continued the legacy of the groundbreaking ProjectDiane research, which has generated billions of media impressions globally for being the first-ever data report on the state of Latina and Black women entrepreneurs in the United States. The former board chair of digitalundivided, Lauren took the helm as CEO to evolve and grow the organization to further support women of color entrepreneurs, especially in the wake of the racial reckoning amid the COVID-19 pandemic. Lauren's career has been shaped by her ability to find opportunities, whether new lines of revenue, ways to squeeze more out of existing profit margins, or ways to enhance a product or deliver more value. That's just how her mind works. It's best summarized as seeing gaps and having the ability to identify and seize hidden profitable value.

When Alison sat down with Lauren to speak about leadership, she had just begun her new role as president of Digital Innovation for Hero Media Inc., where she now leads all lines of business for

17

the company. Hero Media is a Black-owned media and advertising agency that has been around for about four years. The founder and chairman, Joe Anthony, had been a colleague of Lauren's, and she watched him lead some of the greatest campaigns of our time, including the most recent Lenovo campaign. Hero is doing incredible work across the gamut: financial services, products, services, tech, media, entertainment, travel, and health care. In her new role, Lauren gets to do a little bit of everything: running all lines of business, including content, creator partnerships, brand partnerships, agency partnerships, new talent development, tentpole events, upfronts, and their ad tech solution, as well as VC funding and dealing with investors. Lauren shared that her hope for the transition was to be entrepreneurial, to feel and operate like a founder and have the opportunity to build with resources: "I wanted to stay at the intersection of the culture and for the culture: standing up for women of color and using my experiences and network to open doors for people up against similar stereotypes as I have been. I love doing work that changes lives and providing opportunities to creators for visibility, amplification, and to create revenue and monetize their passions."

Currently, everything you see at Hero Media has been built in-house by the agency side. The website, content, tech stack, ad tech solution, and app have all been built-in house the same way Hero Media does for clients. So, while it's still a startup in many ways, Lauren shared how they have more muscle and a foundation she can build on. There are several hundred billion dollars spent annually on global advertising. In the racial reckoning, there was a movement and a call to action for at least 10% of that to be spent with diverse-owned content creators, publishers, and media companies. Even if you take 10% of $200 billion, you get $20 billion. Lauren believes this is a massive business if even a fraction of that can be captured: "The opportunity is to play big in this space and prove why something is needed specifically for the culture. Our proprietary ad tech solution allows us to generate revenue and service advertising partners in a way that many of the bigger publishers can do. We democratize access by allowing diverse creators and publishers to utilize our ad tech software and platform."

There are many ways to drive impact. Leadership within a for-profit business such as media and entertainment differs from the styles and expectations of people working in nonprofit, social justice, and other social impact work. Venture philanthropy is critical, and we often need private-sector talent to solve public interest problems effectively.

Lauren explains, "I gave a keynote speech at the first digitalundivided conference twelve years ago. This was before it was incorporated as a nonprofit, before we had a movement for Black people and women of color within technology, innovation, and the start-up ecosystem. From its inception, I was a cheerleader for the organization, chaired our board of directors until 2020, and then I was unanimously appointed to serve as CEO. Likewise, I inherited Project Diane, a biennial research report named for Diane Nash, one of the first Black female innovators. When I took the reins as CEO, I transformed it substantially, five X'd our revenue from $1 million to $5 million in less than eighteen months by bringing in more than 65 corporate, Fortune 500, and unicorn companies as strategic partners. I increased our programming and the research's frequency, breadth, and scope."

When Lauren was with digitalundivided, she did well there because she didn't come up with a myopic nonprofit viewpoint. Rather than subsisting on grants, they did sponsorships. She rewrote the script in an entrepreneurial way. At Hero Media, Lauren can use different media of content to shine a spotlight and give voice and digital real estate to Black founders. For example, she invested in Partake Cookies, one of the fastest-growing allergen-free baked goods and cookie companies. The founder is a Black and Asian American woman named Denise Woodard. As her company grew, she realized a dearth of Black representation within food and food packaging. Concerned about food sources and our longevity, Partake started a scholarship at Howard specifically for African Americans who want to get into food and food science. This is where Lauren sees leadership heading: companies going out into the world and doing great things with their profits and presence. "Ultimately, I'm a Black woman still subject to the same stereotypes, hardships, doubts, and difficulties of the people I seek to serve. All of us, any group that has had their chance at ascension or success in the last couple of years, rightfully so, have to apply our oxygen mask first."

Reading about Lauren, it is easy to see why so many come to her for advice and mentorship. Mentees will sometimes ask her how to thank their mentors and reciprocate when they are just beginning their careers. Lauren's advice is that many experienced businesspeople need and want to stay relevant, stay in the know, and stay connected—and mentees are often ready to help. "I tell young people to share articles and highlight trends, areas within the culture, media, and whatever is hip and relevant. That's a lot more valuable than your coffee. I call that the Beyoncé effect. Why is Beyoncé still a fan-favorite? Why is she still such an in-demand artist? She stays around the youngest, hippest, up-and-coming rising star artists who write with her, write for her, collaborate with her, produce for her, keep her fresh, and keep her relevant. You can't live in a glass house and then stay connected to the streets."

Leadership can come from anywhere because we all have different experiences that bring value. Lauren has never had one mentor because there's not one person whose life she wants to copy-paste in full. "There are people I admire for one thing and another, and I go to each for what I respect the most about them. Every relationship I've had that resembled a mentorship is, in fact, reciprocal. Many people, especially a lot of women, call me their big little sister or Auntie Lauren; they feel like I have an old soul or a lot of senior experience in the business. They've taught me how to reframe my expectations. They've taught me organization. They've taught me patience, and they've taught me grace."

7

Full Thought Leadership

Dr. Derreck Kayongo is an internationally recognized visionary, humanitarian and, founder of the Global Soap Project: a humanitarian aid organization that collects discarded and unused soap from hotels worldwide, reprocesses it, and then distributes it to in-need populations around the world. His passion for helping others and commitment to innovative thinking led him to the role of CEO of the National Center for Civil and Human Rights. During his time as CEO, he elevated the global visibility of the Center, showcasing stories of victims of civil rights abuse and the heroic actions that changed the course of history. Derreck currently serves on the board of advisors at Sharing Sacred Spaces, an organization devoted to building local, sustainable interreligious communities working together for peace and civic change. A phenomenal speaker and storyteller, Derreck is a leader in both global health and environmental sustainability.

(Highlights from our interview, recorded May 26, 2023.)

I'M FROM UGANDA, A SMALL country in East Africa, which prides itself on many things, especially being the source of the Nile. That's a contested space because Ethiopians also think they're the source of the Nile, but they're not here to talk, so I will take that one. I now live in Atlanta, where a good group of people, who have grown and moved out of the home, call me Dad. I founded the

Global Soap Project about 12 years ago, which takes partially used soap from hotels, the ones you leave behind, and recycles them safely to be reused. I came up with a formula to do that safely and built an organization out of that idea. I'm now training other leaders to think through legacy—how to do things that change the world and leave it a better place.

The truth is we all see a lot of things every day. The things I see, you also see. But do you care about what I see? As a former refugee, when I saw a partially used bar of soap, it meant something to me. I asked the question, "Why are they wasting soap?" If I was wealthy, I probably would have seen used soap and had what my son calls the ick factor. I look brilliant because I picked up on something through the eyes of a refugee, something we can now all agree is a huge waste of resources. Before innovation, you have to see the eyes and who they belong to. I also was not the first person to understand soap was being wasted; my eyes could do something about it because they belonged to a child whose father was a soap maker. I had the tools to do something because I knew what soap was and how it was made. My eyes also belonged to someone whose parents were innovators and entrepreneurs; I saw entrepreneurship take place and be possible. And then, of course, my eyes are also shaped individually. My brothers, who came from the same family, never came up with the idea.

Sometimes ideas visit people who can help put them in place in this world. If you observe and listen enough, go back and spend time with your idea; with hard work and resources, your tool kit will come to life. The Global Soap Project wasn't invented in a day. There's an observation, an idea, and then a lot of time. The idea stuck with me, and I kept adding more tools to the tool kit until I was ready to implement.

One of the tenets of a leader is charisma. A leader has to be able to convince people around them that what they're trying to do is powerful; all it requires from you is to believe. I created a story that made my idea believable and doable; it made people wonder why no one had thought of it yet. Stories are how leaders get people to do courageous things; they have charisma, can sell, make noise, and have a presence. Stories and charisma are especially important in building partnerships.

Years ago, I met Vicky Gordon, who was on the board of an organization I worked for, and we struck up a friendship. Vicky was the vice president of Hilton Hotels, and when I shared my idea for soap, she was excited. As a leader, you can't be quiet. You have to share your ideas with as many people as you can. Our individual partnership was pivotal. Through her relationships and partnerships, she helped me build the board of the Global Soap Project, which included UPS and the Centers for Disease Control, people I would never have known just by being Derreck. I understood the value of a network from my father, that if I met the right person, it would have a ripple effect. Through Vicky, we build corporate partnerships with Hilton and the Hilton Corporation to provide $1.3 million in grant money to build our first factory. When I worked for the development agency Care International, I met Peter, who was in charge of their water and sanitation program. He managed programs to provide clean water to refugees and people in distressed areas. But one thing they didn't have was soap. You can have water, but you can't really clean up without soap. My idea and story played right into their hygiene purposes, and everything started to line up. The process was in different silos, broken down by networking, and I was able to begin connecting them. The Global Soap Project was underway to move into 90 countries worldwide.

A leader needs knowledge to have full thought. South African musician Miriam Makeba said the same thing better: "If you are going to wear blinders, then you do not know the world." A leader with full thought knows Southern poets and philosophers such as

Ngũgĩ wa Thiong'o, who wrote "The River Between" and "The Petals of Blood," or Chinua Achebe. They go to the Middle East and find Rumi and Confucius in the East. What began as a thought in England, by the time it circles the globe and gets you to Asia and to Confucius, has a different meaning. It has different accommodations as a thought and different representations of humanity as a thought; therefore, those representations create a different capaciousness to allow new injections to make it lively and more recognizable as it travels from you as the leader of that thought. Today's leaders read too much on the Western side of their thought as leaders, and therefore they're not recognizable by the time they get to Shanghai, to Palestine, to Mesopotamia. Crossing information and obtaining new knowledge is vital, as is an understanding of Southern forms of leadership. Beyond knowledge, leaders need wisdom. Wisdom is more, what we might call emotional intelligence. Think of the ocean. It's fed by rivers, lakes, by water from every corner of the earth. The ocean never says no; it takes the water in no matter where it comes from and creates a whole universe, an ecosystem, which contains good, bad, and everything in between. The ocean doesn't penalize or judge; it gathers. Leaders with both wisdom and knowledge are truly extraordinary.

You can read the *7 Habits of Highly Successful People*, but are there just seven? Or is it 20? It may only be two—the two lessons to be a highly effective Derreck. There are never steps for everyone. Learn from others, but collect your own narrative. Learn how to play, and work less or study less. For me, that balance is to work hard and also travel. Learn how to cook or how to raise an animal; have hobbies that go to the core of who you are. Take all that, the lessons, the stories, and your passions, and create an acronym for yourself. What is your metaphor? SELF is an acronym I use to govern who I am on earth: service, education, leadership, and faith. I should be in service to others to gain recognition. Service requires education, knowing what you're good at, and getting better because you learn new stories and gain knowledge while in service. Being in service and continually learning makes you a leader. Not necessarily a leader for everybody but a leader of self. When you can lead yourself well, others will follow. Faith is not just a religious form of faith but faith in myself and others' ability to have faith in me. Can people trust me to handle situations with grace?

Every young leader should make mistakes as much as possible because they can be more expensive when you're older. Through mistakes, you learn, especially when you are intentional about it. Make mistakes, and go into your reflective nature; see what happened and why. Then, as my dad used to say, you can come back and make better mistakes that move the ball forward. Value and build your network. Be observant about who you meet along your journey because they may become important down the road. Gather their stories, as many as possible along your way; they become some of the best influences in your life. Learn from them because stories are teachers.

8

Leadership Has Your Back

OUR UNDERSTANDING OF LEADERSHIP IS often shaped by the leaders who have taught, supported, and inspired us along the way. When I think about leadership, I think about the people who have your back and recognize your hard work. I'm **Scott Stratten**, and I've had a lot of jobs. I worked at McDonalds, but it's no longer there now. It was demolished. Not my fault. Then I worked at Red Lobster, where our veterinarian's office is now. Not my fault. Worked at a Famous Players movie theatre, which is a Staples now. Not my fault. Sports Authority was next; I sold fishing gear. They went bankrupt and left the country, which certainly isn't my fault. I was also a waiter for a while at Opera Emporium. That didn't close down, though; it burned down. I promise it wasn't my fault.

My favorite job was working at the movie theatre. I was a triple threat—a terrible box office attendant, a lazy usher, and a not-so-trustworthy candy concession worker. The theatre had a softball team, and I was hired as a ringer (I went zero for six in our first game, if you're wondering how that turned out). I didn't see eye to eye with any of my managers, especially our general manager, whose name I won't share—okay, her name was Brenda. In hindsight,

27

95% of the problem was me. I'd come in at six for a shift that started at six, punch in, and hang out in the staff room. My 15-minute breaks always took at least 20 or 25 minutes. I gave away shifts and would then come in and watch a movie after giving them away (bold!). All Brenda wanted was for me to do the job I was hired for, but to me that was a big ask.

One day, I was sweeping up at the concession. *Forrest Gump* was playing, and I remember it vividly because the movie was so popular, and the place was packed. A woman burst through the doors of the Majestic Theatre and headed straight toward me. A minute or so before, a kid had come out asking for a large cup of water. Now, the concession stand has rules, and we weren't allowed to give the large cups of water because they were counted for inventory. So I gave him one of the tiny water cups the theatre let us serve (with a smile and an attitude). Unimpressed, he told me off and went back to the theatre. Apparently, he was going for backup.

His mom was angry. She came right up to the stand and started yelling at me. My wisdom at the time told me to start throwing it back. I knew I'd probably lose my job, but I figured if I was going to go down, it would be like Bon Jovi, in a blaze of glory. We were yelling at one another, when I felt a hand on my shoulder. It wasn't forceful; it was almost like a warm glow. The hand guided me backward (I think I heard angels singing), and there was Brenda. She slowly moved me back and put herself between me and the customer. Brenda looked at the woman and said, "Lady, get out of my theatre. You don't talk to people that way. You don't talk to Scott that way. Who do you think you are? Go get your refund. Take your kid and never come back." She then escorted them out and returned to ask if I was okay. Brenda told me she had my back, and more importantly, she showed me.

Brenda gave me one of my first leadership lessons: leadership is about action. Leaders need to have their teams' backs, and it can't just be written or talked about. As a snarky 17-year-old, I didn't set the concession stand rules, and Brenda knew that. She took accountability and didn't throw me under the bus. I did a complete 180 at work after that. I went from an employee who thought everybody was against me to someone who knew their boss had their back. I showed up on time, took appropriate breaks, and realized other people had to pick up the slack when I was late. A year or two later, Brenda told me how I'd become one of her best employees when I was fired for theft (just kidding, I was going to college, and they never caught me). She turned everything around for me by having my back; I've never forgotten that.

Once Brenda won me over and changed my brain, I got really into working at the theatre. My coworkers were awesome and are still some of my best friends today. At the time, studios sent theatres stuff they could use to promote new movies; we called them Standees, big stands with promotional posters and things. My friends and I started doing movie promotions and taking them to the next level, and our managers were behind us. We'd dress up and paint the big bay windows for movies such as *The Nightmare Before Christmas* and *Super Mario Brothers*. We would come in as a group on our own time, seventeen-, eighteen-, and nineteen-year-olds volunteering to promote studio films because we had so much fun together. We went all out when *Maverick* came out (a kind of poker, gambling, Wild West movie; you should see it, so good). We painted the windows with poker cards, teamed up with a local laser tag company, and organized the Fastest Draw in Oakville, where people could win gift cards. We went to Value Village for costumes and dressed up for the opening night. We even organized a charity casino and traded movie passes for big spinning wheels and crown and anchor games. The promotion was in the newspaper, and the media came. We were even threatened with a lawsuit from someone who said they were the fastest draw in Oakville. But they weren't talking about laser guns.

Management came to us and asked to take all the media clippings and photos of the stuff we were doing to send to head office. They really felt the work we were doing was incredible and wanted to share it. We put together a big project binder with all the photos, went to Office Depot, bound it, and sent it to Famous Players' head office. Months went by, and nothing. We received a package back six months later and gathered around, excited to open it. Inside was our binder, with a big check mark on the cover. And that was it. There wasn't even a sticker. It would have meant everything to us to get a little praise or celebration. Other than never sending the binder back at all, it was absolutely the least they could do.

My experience at Famous Players shaped the kind of leader I wanted to become. When Brenda stepped in front of me that day, I felt seen and valued, and it made all the difference. The lack of recognition from head office did just the opposite; I can only imagine the cool things our team would have done for the company if we'd felt our contribution mattered. Leadership is about giving recognition. We all want to feel valued at work; no leader or company's success is a one-person job.

9

Game-Changing Leadership

Orlando Bowen is a game changer and a messenger of hope who inspires change with his words and delivers results with his actions. A keynote speaker, Orlando teaches companies to use forgiveness as a high-performance tool as well as team building and overcoming adversity. He is a speaker, mentor, and the founder and executive director at One Voice, One Team Youth Leadership Organization. His enthusiasm for and commitment to empowering others to get off the sidelines and become difference makers on their teams and in the lives of those around them is contagious.

(Highlights from our interview, recorded May 29, 2023.)

SOME FOLKS SEE LEADERSHIP AS a title or position, but you can lead from anywhere if you show up in a way that honors people. At One Voice, One Team, we encourage young people to do what they can to serve. Sometimes they say, "I don't come from means, Mr. Orlando, I don't have a lot to offer." And we tell them, "You have more than you realize. You are not alone; we're going to lead together." Leadership is about doing what we can with what we have. We often talk about "Ubuntu," a word rooted in the Zulu language that means "I am because we are." When we look at life through this lens of our shared humanity, so much is possible, and leadership becomes how

31

we show up in ways that honor and defend that shared humanity. We often talk about what it means to show up in restorative ways, Afro Indigenous and Indigenous ways of connecting, healing, and being in community. Relationships are the key to creating real possibilities and seeing change within people. You have to show up and resist the thought of engaging people from a deficit perspective. Some people ask, "When it comes to the notion of restorative practice or restorative justice, what are we restoring to?" These questions are often asked because these inequalities have existed for millennia. We are restoring to what we're innately wired to be—in community. The world doesn't have to be win or lose—it would be win, win, win. And that's what we seek to create—spaces that are win, win, win.

We run a summer program called SWOLE Camp (Self-respect, Work hard, Overcome adversity, Lead by example, and Excellence). In camp, we talk about what it means to lead by example. Peer-to-peer learning like this is so powerful. The facilitators lead the conversation, and also tap into the wisdom right in the room. Leaders build strong teams by showing up in ways that edify, celebrate, and honor. They show others they belong to something bigger than themselves. That's why we focus on community and on that energy. We do a dance we call the breakdown, where we rock from side to side. It's about seeing each other; there is no beginning, end, or hierarchy. In that moment, we can let go and commit ourselves to something greater than ourselves. That is team to me—how can I show up for you today? How can I serve? I want to set the tone in terms of what's possible from a leadership perspective.

Leadership is the relentless drive to make sure you can care for those you're responsible to and for, something my parents modeled for me. Growing up as immigrants, we didn't have much in terms of materialistic things. My parents worked hard to keep a roof over our heads and food on the table. They never spoke about the struggles and the hardships, and so growing up, I had no idea what we were going through as a family. Now, as an adult, and after having many conversations with my parents about the struggle, I now have a greater understanding and appreciation for how much the adults in our family sacrificed so we have a chance. My grandparents were always about the community win. They celebrated every kid's accomplishment and taught me what community looks like. It wasn't only the big things; it was in small moments of knowing and honoring others, celebrating victories big and small. You could see the impact on the faces of the young people in our community because if one of us won in the community, we all won. They instilled a sense of belief in terms of possibilities and understanding the importance of community.

As a parent, I see leadership as helping our kids find their path, to help them be positive, contributing members of their communities who to use their gifts and talents to make a difference in the world. My father-in-law, Chuck Ealey, a CFL and NCAA football legend, was just inducted into the 2022 College Football Hall of Fame. He holds the record for the most consecutive wins by any NCAA starting quarterback, 35-0. When our boys hear those stats and see that level of recognition, they see the end product, the win streak, and as we all celebrate the end product, the undefeated win streak, we highlight the process that led there and some of the things Chuck had to navigate in the process. As he was leading a record-setting team, their grandfather faced tremendous struggle. His mom was struggling financially, and his five-year-old brother was dying of cancer, to name a couple. When folks ask him, "How'd you win 35 games?" he always answers, "One play at a time." That's why Mr. Ealey, aka the Wizard of Oohs and Ahhs, exuded calm and coolness under pressure—one play at a time and never gave up. When you focus on the play in front of you, you don't worry about things you can't control.

When I ask the kids in our community, "What if you could wave this magic wand? What would you want people to understand about you?" they want us to know they aren't selfish; they're just trying to figure things out. That the world is changing quickly, and things are different for them. They want to be recognized and honored and not discounted because of their age or appearance. They want adults to stay open to learning and be open about their own challenges and vulnerabilities. In a recent conversation with a group of high school youth, they shared that it's not cool to be happy right now, to bring energy and celebrate at school. So we keep celebrating and sharing joy because young people need that. We create a space where young people can be however they are, accepted and celebrated.

One of the most important things we try to espouse is that we never arrive at leadership. It is a process of iteration and reinvention. If we stay humble, there is always learning we can benefit from. Stay open and recognize you can learn from anyone. Don't discount people because of title, socioeconomic background, or appearance. Look at people from a lens of shared humanity, and lead in ways that honor and serve humanity in every interaction.

Leadership and legacy aren't about what you say; it's about how you show up to that one play right in front of you.

10

Leadership Closes the Gap

Megan McDonald is the senior vice president of Single-Family Sales at MCAP, Canada's largest independent mortgage financing company, with annual sales exceeding $14 billion and over $75 billion in assets under administration. There, she manages the direction of sales for two flagship brands, MCAP and Eclipse. MCAP is also a client; at the time of writing, UnMarketing was leading the Entrepreneurs in Residence program for MCAP mortgage brokers.

(Highlights from our interview, recorded May 22, 2023.)

FROM A LEADERSHIP STANDPOINT, ONE of the greatest gifts I can bring to my team is belief in the company, our direction, and them. I've had opportunities in my career to work with different leaders and have resonated most with those with the greatest belief in the company and its direction. Not the company as in the logo but belief in the people and their choices. These leaders clarified the reasons behind decisions and communicated why I mattered to the direction we were going. When you believe in what you're doing, have passion, and convey that to others by setting the standard and tone, you have a better chance of working collaboratively.

A leadership tool kit might encompass reward and recognition, challenge and skill development, and the word most people like to avoid—criticism. I am here to inspire, create direction, and help improve people's lives. As leaders, we don't have just accountability; we have responsibility. People often want a title for accountability because they want to be in charge and take control. If you genuinely want to support people, you offer them the best advice, and you don't care what the outcome is because if you do, that's control. True support is creating a safe environment that's fun and encouraging and allows people to be the best at what they do. It doesn't come with strings attached.

Coming up the ranks, I noticed this interesting way of doing reviews. You counted everything everybody did right and they did wrong, and then you put it on a piece of paper and presented it to them; you had to take a U-Haul of your failures and drag it around for the rest of your career. With my teams, I promise that nothing will end on their year-end review if it is resolved. That encourages risk, failure, and innovation. If you're in a leadership role, you aren't just there to share the reward—you're there to share the risk. Leading by example is critical. Many people want their teams to be more respectful, but you have to model that for your team. Do you embody being on time? Do you embody taking responsibility? Do you embody respect and apologize for your own mistakes? Too many leaders are afraid to say they're sorry. As a leader, I don't expect to do other people's jobs, nor do they expect me to do so. They do expect me to bleed when they bleed, have the same challenges, and set the standard.

When faced with challenging conversations, I always go back to an analogy about the weather—there's no good or bad weather, just weather. There are no good or bad conversations; there are just conversations. Avoiding discomfort is leadership avoidance; it's letting things continue you know are not right because you don't know how to handle it. When you build a culture of trust and transparency, your ability to have difficult conversations improves dramatically. I live by the philosophy that there is room for forgiveness if you speak your truth with grace. I don't sell perfection; I sell partnership. When I am in the service of others, the money comes, the reward comes, and the recognition comes. From early in my career, I've believed that my clients and everyone I worked with and for were my partners. I have had this beautiful opportunity at MCAP over the years, where I've been able to work on both sides of the business. Clients don't see us as separate teams, so our work should be fluid and transparent. Leadership in both areas has to be in it to win it together. I am responsible for appreciating other teams and advocating for and complimenting them. We often think reward and recognition are top-down, but they should be all around—up, sideways, everywhere. When you demonstrate that behavior regardless of title, everyone begins to believe in a greater client experience.

Business is personal. When you try to break those two apart, authenticity, vulnerability, care, and grace go out the window. My father was an entrepreneur; he owned a construction company as a developer. I would always go to his office and meet his business partners; he had four. When we would leave and get to the parking lot, all these partners would get into their Mercedes, Porsches, and BMWs. And there was my dad, with our Honda Accord. Even though he had four partners, my father was the leader of this company. So one day, when I got in the car, I asked him, "Why do you drive such a crappy car?" He replied, "I don't drive a crappy car. Honda Accord's a great car, Megan. It's got great gas mileage. It's never let me down. This Honda Accord has 420,000 kilometers on it, Megan. And guess what? When I drive up to my job site, my workers are there, and I'm not one foot away from my people. When these gentlemen drive up to the job site, they're twenty feet away the minute they drive up. I can't afford to be twenty feet away from my people, because the distance between me and them is going to happen naturally from my title, my position. I don't want to add to it." As a leader, every time you make a decision, I want you to ask yourself, "Am I putting another foot between me and my people, or am I closing the gap?"

11

Leadership Is a Group Project

AWARENESS ISN'T ALWAYS COMFORTABLE BECAUSE you often have to reevaluate your values and practices. But when you value the voices and contributions of others, you build relationships and create strong teams and partnerships. Rather than focusing on their own successes, UnLeaders are about the team win. The vast majority of North American CEOs and CFOs believe improving company culture would boost financial performance and recognize their organizational culture is not as healthy as it could be (Graham et al. 2016). Between aspiration (what work could be) and reality (what work actually is) we find leadership—by far the most important factor in improving workplace environments. Toxic workplaces are costly, with workers more likely to report anxiety and burnout. Leadership is consistently the best predictor of culture, and solutions focus on behavior, social norms, and work design. To change corporate culture, we need more than a quick fix or training—we need sustained interventions over time and leadership at every level.

Research shows relationships are fundamental to leadership. A 2018 Udemy study found that nearly half of employees surveyed had quit because of a bad manager, and almost two-thirds believed their manager lacked proper managerial training (Udemy 2018). The study offered three critical areas to improve: communication, psychological safety, and proving growth opportunities. The issue is this: you can't improve skills such as communication or understand team safety and aspirations without relationships. Communication doesn't exist in a vacuum—it is relational. You can't create growth opportunities without knowing your team, and you certainly can't create safety without understanding and accountability.

The "State of the Global Workplace Report" found that only 21% of employees are engaged at work and only 33% say they're thriving in their overall well-being (Gallup 2023). That leaves the majority disengaged and stressed out. We spend so much of our lives working or at work; if you're unhappy at work, the rest of your life suffers. Leaders sit in a position to make change—to improve not only their own mindset but that of their teams. Awareness is the beginning, but there's a lot more to do. Leadership requires decentering yourself, listening, taking feedback, and empathy. Empathy is about others—recognizing that like you, everyone brings all their stuff to work too. It's about seeing the human in another, not treating workers like numbers. Humility takes awareness and empathy and allows you to understand you walk a path others have walked and need the knowledge/experience of others to take ideas and create action.

12

Leadership Is a Mindset-Based on Practice

WHEN WE UNDERSTAND LEADERSHIP BEYOND title, it emerges as a transferable tool kit of curiosity, vision, communication, and confidence. Few people demonstrate this better than **Jeff Adams**, a Canadian Paralympian, six-time world champion in wheelchair racing, and Osgoode Hall Law School graduate. Born in Brampton, Ontario, Jeff underwent radiation therapy to treat cancer as an infant, which saved his life but permanently damaged his spinal cord. Learning to use his wheelchair as a piece of athletic equipment, Jeff discovered new ways to fulfil his potential. He rose to elite levels of competition on the international stage and became one of Canada's most successful Paralympic athletes. Jeff has served as a spokesperson, journalist, and media commentator, as well as chair of the Accessibility Committee for the Toronto 2008 Olympic Bid Committee and chair of the Ontarians with Disability Advisory Council. After retiring from competition, he transitioned from sport to business, founding two medical device engineering companies, which he sold in 2016 to return to school to study law. He was called to the Ontario Bar in June 2021 and is currently working at Fasken LLP, a Bay Street law firm specializing in management-side

41

labor and employment and human rights law. In 2018 Jeff was inducted into Canada's Sports Hall of Fame.

The common thread in Jeff's work, the North Star, is to help people. As an athlete, he was given a platform, an amplified voice, and he used this to talk about social issues he cares about— accessibility, disability rights, and human rights. After retiring from sport, his catalyst to start two medical device engineering companies was wanting to give people access to significantly better technology and make medical devices, including wheelchairs, that could change people's lives for the better. When those businesses ended, he embarked on a career in law and now works to ensure access to justice and provide support to ensure his clients' legal rights are protected.

These might seem like radical changes, but Jeff told us they happened slowly. "As an amateur athlete in Canada, you market yourself, sign endorsement contracts, arrange deals, get to vital races, manage your money, buy equipment, and ensure your equipment stays up to date. I used transferable skills in contracts, supply chain, and procurement as I was transitioning to business. I'd been doing elements of business for 20 years and transferred those skills into a start-up that aligned with my values. With law, I managed the legal work in my business, pulling contracts, liaising with patent lawyers, and providing instructions to counsel for patents and some of the financing. Realizing how much I loved the legal side of the business led me to law school."

Change is good; the more gradual the change, the easier, more effective, and efficient. When Jeff told his friends he would work at a Bay Street law firm, many were surprised, but to Jeff, it was a chance to work from the inside and talk to corporations about how to do things the right way. He writes anti-violence and -harassment policies for some of the biggest corporations in Canada, an amazing opportunity to affect change from the inside. Accessibility in the disability context means opening doors and making places, programs, and opportunities available to the most people you can. Jeff says that in terms of leadership, it's the same—"creating opportunities, ideas, concepts, and projects open and available to as many people as possible, which starts with making yourself as open and available as possible. If you aren't open and available to people, you can't be a leader; it's antithetical."

Some of Jeff's work is around terminations, companies downsizing or having to lay off or terminate with their restructuring or acquisition. It is hard for everybody, but Jeff says there is a way to do it correctly; there are legal requirements—you can't pay women a different rate, you can't fire people for reasons prohibited by law, you have to comply with the accessibility laws. And ultimately, there is a real business case for doing things the right way. Jeff often deals with many allegations of human rights breaches, which are defended vigorously when necessary, and in circumstances where he can advise on how to avoid similar circumstances in the future, he does. "We've got good laws in Canada for equity and justice from an employment standards perspective, especially in Ontario. Helping companies work within those legislative protections is a big and valuable part of my job."

Whether in sport, business, law, or life, Jeff believes success as a leader means recognizing and celebrating the value of your team. Strong teams are especially important during times of uncertainty. No one likes uncertainty, but it can be a huge opportunity. If you have confidence in your skills when things are uncertain, those with confidence are more likely to be successful. Jeff reminded himself of that as an athlete and actually tried to cultivate chaos to the detriment of his competitors. Of course, he doesn't do it purposely anymore, but when he recognizes uncertainty or chaos, he tries to remind himself that this is what he's been preparing for. "Practice allows you to create true confidence rather than a veneer or a "fake it till you make it" attitude. "As an athlete or a lawyer, a big part of my job is being able to tell when someone else is faking it. Whether it is a witness or opposing counsel, you can tell when someone isn't ready, they haven't done their homework, they don't have the facts, they don't know the law—whatever it is. True confidence is a mindset based on practice."

Jeff believes that, like confidence, resilience takes practice. An athlete doesn't parachute into the Olympics or Paralympics; you train to face up to whatever barrier is in front of you. You have opportunities to turn the dial and gradually increase the intensity of the barrier, whether real or artificial, and the resilience you need to overcome it. You don't always have that graduated approach in business, but you can find ways to practice resilience. Jeff shares that "resilience is a transferable skill as long as you recognize it as a skill in development. It is a fallacy to think we can constantly self-motivate. That's one of the reasons athletes have coaches; a big part of their job is keeping the athlete motivated. The same applies to resilience—you can't always find it alone. As an athlete, you need the best people in place and to trust them. Even in an individual sport, you have a team that got you there. You get the best coach, training partners, physiotherapist, doctor, and manager; surround yourself with the team and rely on them daily. In business, although I was CEO, the face of the company, and did almost everything, I assembled the best team of accountants, engineers, warehouse managers, and supply chain experts, and I relied on them. As a lawyer, I'm often in court addressing the justice, judge or arbitrator, as the case may be, but I have law clerks, students, colleagues, and research lawyers behind all the work. It can be difficult to ask for help or rely on others because of pride, but it is critical to have a support network in place, to let them make the sounds of support for you on days when you need to hear it. None of us get to our finish lines alone."

13

The Leadership Gap

As LONG AS THERE'S BEEN a younger generation, an older one has told them they've ruined things. For a while, it was millennials getting the flack; now it's Gen Z, labeled as lazy, without loyalty, disconnected from the "real" in-person world, walking around with their TikToks; apparently this is the end of the civilized world as we know it. Endless articles have been written about how to tame these generations. How do we get them in line? Get them to pay their dues? How do we get them to be more like us old folks? We're a bit tired of discussing the generation gap and how that affects leadership. We'd prefer not having to convince you that your coworkers and employees, no matter their ages, bring unique value to your business, and deserve a voice, fair treatment at work, and the same opportunities for well-being and challenge. UnLeadership is about stepping away from a deficit mentality and seeing the value of each individual. New ideas and challenges to "how things have always been" are opportunities to lead, educate, plant seeds, and raise up the next generation of leaders.

Gen Z was born into a digital world; many of our generation (Gen X) gave them their first iPads. They're witnessing climate change and social justice movements in real time and have seen the growth of social enterprise. In the US, Gen Z represents 26.5% of the population. Although currently a smaller percentage of leadership in the workforce, that is changing and will continue to change over time. Although the average CEO is around 55 today, in 2023 a third of newly appointed S&P 500 CEOs last year were younger than 50, which is more than twice the rate in 2018 (McKinsey & Company 2023). None of us like to be grouped together by decade, and generations aren't necessarily all the same. However, data shows that Gen Z are educated and diverse and by and large inclusive, progressive, and comfortable with technology when compared to their older counterparts (The Annie E. Casey Foundation 2023). Gen Z will be shaping the future of work, and research shows that emerging generations believe effective leadership is result-driven and focused on service; leaders are emotionally intelligent, prioritize team needs, and focus on consistency and transparency in communication. They're worried about climate change, want to work for ethical companies, and feel their efforts matter. They don't want to waste time, be discounted or overlooked, and they want to feel safe and supported at work. Sounds a lot like the rest of us, too.

The difference is for younger generations, the stakes of making change are higher. Alison spoke with content producer and political social commentator Corey Andrew Powell to learn more about leadership and Gen Z. *Corey has spent his career analyzing media and works directly with future leaders at The National Society of Leadership and Success (NSLS), where he hosts the Motivational Mondays podcast. What follows are highlights from our interview, October 19, 2023.*

Gen Z is the first generation born completely into a digital space. A lot of us were sort of on the cusp, so we had to learn to navigate and adjust. On one hand, corporations and society in general look to this generation as the great savior from a technological standpoint, but at the same time Gen Z has a distinct way in which they view their role in corporate society. They have decided that what their parents tolerated is no longer going to work for them. They don't want your cubicle, your lunch break—and, it's not arrogance; Gen Z is saying they're going to do the work on their own terms. Their grasp of technology is one of the great attributes of this generation. This is a competency for them. Beyond their understanding, they have the ability to really take that technology and make it digestible for other people. I believe the issue we are having is with gatekeepers, people from older generations in the corporate environment, who are seemingly inflexible when it comes to dealing with Gen Z. There needs to be a compromise between tangible experience and innovation.

Gen Z is a very socially conscious demographic regarding what they will demand of brands, organizations, and businesses. They push for corporate responsibility and want a different world than their parents had. They bring a genuine passion for "Hey, can we do things differently?" Most of them have completely thrown out the old nine-to-five work structure. They are more interested in hybrid and remote work models and less interested in old-fashioned ideas about dress codes and "professional attire." Let's say you're looking for a financial planner for your retirement. I have this one guy over here who is a master—he's made millions for his clients who are retiring comfortably, based on sound investments. He's also doing the work in sweatpants and flip-flops. Now, there's another guy in his Brooks Brothers suit. He looks amazing; his shoes are polished, and his hair is cut. Honey, he even smells good. But he's also got 15 clients suing him for financial incompetency because he's squandered their investments. When I give you a choice between these two to manage your money, does the suit make a difference in their competency? At the end of the day, that exterior is a costume, and we are all wearing one. It means nothing about my abilities.

The entire world is stacked against Gen Z in many ways, so avoiding resistance and activism is almost impossible. Without fighting back, members of Gen Z may not even be able to have a stable adulthood, let alone a chance to pursue careers, dreams, or other lifestyles that previous generations took for granted. There is a sense that Gen Z needs to take action and do something before time runs out. Combined with being deeply passionate about modern social issues, this trait is fanning the flames of revolutionary energy. Gen Z leaders are guiding the way through compelling storytelling, leading from the front lines instead of hierarchically and their willingness to put justice ahead of personal gain. Young people are organizing protests, just like past generations—like the most famous generation for protest, the 1960s. They are doing advocacy. Look at the Parkland shooting, and what came out of that. These kids are now on the national stage of politics, advocating for gun safety and more gun restrictions. I mean, my God, they've been shot at, these kids. They grew up when you went to school and had to go through metal detectors because you might get killed. They want to lead themselves out of that because they've had enough. That all takes leadership. Not seeing leadership in Gen Z is inaccurate and a terrible assessment."

Corey's advice to aspiring leaders is to let your work speak for itself:

"My first time being given the opportunity to be a manager was when I was hired as a copywriter for a national brand. It was myself and another writer who was not keeping up. As a copywriting team, I picked up a lot of the slack while they were on Facebook and shopping online. I was promised to become a manager, but it needed to happen sooner. So I kept running into my boss's office and saying so-and-so isn't doing their work, and so-and-so is upsetting me for not doing their job. Finally, probably because I was annoying her, my boss told me to stop. She said, "Listen, you won't get the promotion based on what someone else isn't doing. You will get the promotion based on what you are doing." And that was all she had to say. If I went out and did the work, it would be undeniable—it would speak for itself. A month later, the situation was resolved, and I was a manager for the first time with my own team of copywriters I could hire. Understanding that one component changed my life."

14

UnLeadership, Trust, and Community

When a snowstorm hit the University of Kentucky campus, students went online to share their snow stories, and Devan Dannelly decided to see whether he could get out of class the next day. He tweeted to the university president, offering a deal—if the dean would come and dig out his driveway, Devan would go to class. If you're the president of a large university and one of your students tweets this to you, what do you do? You could undoubtedly ignore him, or maybe you have an automated reply for all tweets to you, something like, "Thank you for reaching out. Please call the Office of the President at . . ." Well, Michael Benson decided to go a different way. He replied that Devan had a deal and asked for his address, promptly shoveling the driveway and posing for a photo with Devan's mom and dog. Not only did Devan get to class promptly from then on, but the pictures and story also went viral.

We absolutely love this story because President Benson is fun and kind and takes the time to connect with his students. We love it because he uses his students' communication tools (in this case, Twitter) to reply and show Devan that he is valued as part of the college community and as a person. This wasn't a community-building campaign or a one-time thing; Mr. Benson's Twitter feed is full of amazing photos of him with happy students excited to meet him. The best part of the story is how it inspired others to connect and help one another. Leadership like President Benson's creates community and loyalty—the best defense against the storm, whether that is an actual storm or the fast-paced change in the age of disruption.

In *UnMarketing* and *UnSelling* we wrote about the trust gap and the hierarchy of buying, sharing how to position your brand so that when people are in the market for your product or service, you are their obvious go-to. A huge part of that is trust. Any purchase comes with risk, and the greater the purchase, the more trust that is needed to close the gap. Loyalty is based on trust, and leaders who serve—and value and facilitate community—are best suited to lead their companies through uncertainty. We don't earn trust in one act, with one good idea or presentation—we earn trust by showing up authentically as ourselves over time. Leadership is about consistency. The more uncertain the time, the greater the shift or transformation and the bigger the idea—the more trust you need to bridge the gap between you and those you want to lead. Trust is a leader's currency; they work on building and nurturing it and understand it isn't a renewable resource.

15

Rising Leadership

Rachel Wyman is an award-winning baker, trainer, author, and successful entrepreneur. Owner of Rabble Rise Bakery, runner, and CDO (chief doughnut officer), Rachel has a storied history in bread baking and recipe creation for major bakeries. She's an award-winning doughnut baker, with a passion for dough, a knack for flavor, and a talent for innovation.
(Highlights from our interview, recorded June 10, 2023.)

WHEN I OPENED MY BAKERY, I wanted people to feel like it was an extension of their home, a place they wanted to be. That way, if one day the doughnuts suck because of the humidity or something like that, they'll still come back. When my kids were young, there were only a few places to go out and eat and feel comfortable taking them. So we designed a big patio space out front of the bakery that's spacious and safe so young families feel welcome. It has become a vibrant community area. I believe in creating spaces where people can meet and gather, and I have a space. None of this was created to make money; for me, it's about providing access.

Years ago, I noticed tons of runners at the bakery lining up for donuts. I learned carb loading before a race was a thing, created a space for them at the bakery, and launched a 5K fun run. After the success of the first run, a friend who was a runner helped me make it an official 5K race with a measured course and timing. The following year, we aimed to get 250 runners, but in two days, we had 500 people sign up! I was in the middle of moving into a new space about half a block away. We were still waiting for new equipment; I wasn't sure if I could make enough doughnuts for that many people. We had to call the registration company to get them to stop signing people up! In the end, we had 750 runners. I was also one of those first-time runners, and I just kept running; 11 months later, I completed the New York City Marathon. The run is now going into its 10th year and sells out regularly in under four hours to 3,000 runners. One of the coolest parts has been learning that over 60% of our participants are first-time runners. Adding doughnuts, the whimsy, and the fun makes running more approachable. We started a running club, Fueled by Donuts, to give people a place to build their running with other people who are non-runners or coming out for the first time.

Every time I partner with someone, they complement my skill set. My partner for the 5K was someone who had managed big events before. I have people who work on the creative end and are good with budgeting and planning. The key to partnerships is being comfortable accepting positive feedback or criticism. All the key people I've had on my team in leadership roles aren't afraid to call me out or challenge my ideas. One cool partnership I've been a part of is working with Lululemon as a brand ambassador. They look for community leaders who support other people and recognize that person probably needs to be supported better on their own. Our local store reached out to me because of my community development, and I was able to participate in their leadership training, everything that the company makes available to their managers. Their vision and goal programs gave me and my staff a tool kit, which has been huge in helping me grow and feel supported. I recently completed my time with them and was brought back for another four years as a legacy ambassador.

Being a business owner can feel like you're on a lonely island with no one else to share your experience with. I value connecting with other entrepreneurs, someone on an island on the other side of the ocean, by themselves also. Media experiences, being on cooking shows or interviewed for national publications, and speaking at events for other bakers or business owners are all incredible opportunities to make connections. I want people starting out to know they aren't alone, because I wish I had that support. There might be another baker down the block with a smaller mailing list, but she still experiences all the same things I am. It's my social responsibility to use my voice.

When the news about COVID began circulating, I was on my way home from a conference in Chicago; it was the second week of March. The airport had a few masks, but the whole thing hadn't set in yet. School was canceled two days after getting home; it happened so fast. Where we live and work, there were no supply issues; there were supply chain issues. I had no problem getting all the foods I needed to make bread, groceries and fruits and vegetables. I had complete and total access to that, but my community didn't. We adjusted our menu of fancy doughnuts to make "depression donuts," as I called them, four basic flavors. I started baking bread and sold more in those next six months than I've sold in my entire career. We began providing our community with fruits and vegetables. We ensured my staff had fruits, vegetables, eggs, milk, toilet paper, and anything they needed to avoid going to the grocery stores themselves.

At the bakery, we create monthly menus as a team; everyone has input. As soon as one menu is launched, we start working on the next one. We begin with a digital chalkboard where everyone pitches their ideas, from the bakers to retail staff to the teenagers who work a few hours a week. I am transparent about everything, from finances to our recipes. I don't want to keep things a secret because I want someone to take over for me one day. The only way for them to do that is if I give them the resources. I spent a lot of my time teaching others and sharing what I know, and I was recently hired as a professor at the Culinary Institute of America; I started five days ago. We do lots of classes at the bakery for adults and kids. People think yeast is scary, and it doesn't have to be. Guess that makes me the un-baker.

16

Leading for Impact

Paul Taylor is a long-time activist, nonprofit leader, educator, media commentator, and cofounder and principal consultant of Evenings & Weekends Consulting. He is also a professor who teaches organizational leadership, people resources, and fundraising at Simon Fraser University. From 2017 to 2023, Paul served as the executive director of FoodShare Toronto, Canada's largest food justice organization.
(Highlights from our interview, recorded June 5, 2023.)

MY LENS AND THE FOCUS of my work have been challenging poverty and income inequality. What we're paid for our work communicates a lot. Organizations can have all kinds of programs and initiatives, but at the end of the day, people are coming to work largely because they need to pay for things. Many leaders have leaned into programs that require less investment than raising the floor on income levels. Often, these initiatives are inaccessible; leadership communicates a lack of concern for those on the lowest income levels. Organizational leaders should think long and hard about the messaging conveyed through their acceptance of inadequate wages.

In the absence of meaningful government action, it's up to leaders to do what's right to help create healthy communities and individuals. We live in one of the richest places in the world; we have an opportunity to engage in conversations around big ideas to inspire people toward change. Patriarchy, in particular, has informed people's ideas on leadership; leaders have to know all the things and appear decisive and firm. The most liberating thing for me is admitting I don't know; I need to consult people smarter than me to ensure we make good decisions. If we apply our values and are comfortable and confident in those values, we can mitigate the stress of navigating uncertainty. In my work at FoodShare, when inflation was skyrocketing and folks were struggling, we gave everyone a 7% increase. That communicates care more than any program for employee wellness. Leading with your values through uncertainty tells people the ship is being steered well, even though the waters might be choppy. Leadership takes place in the complex ecosystems of relationships we call organizations. Applying a systems-thinking lens to your leadership practice is critical in these times of complexity and uncertainty. People should pay more attention to the power they have to effect positive, systemic change in their communities, teams, and organizations.

The leaders I've looked up to are often people who are uncelebrated, unrecognized, whose names you'll never hear in any books. These are predominantly Black and Indigenous women who I've had the opportunity to learn from. I think about my mom and the leadership she displayed when it came to community care. It's about caring and our interconnected role, especially toward those who have been made most vulnerable. My grandmother Maisie was poor but believed kids were the future and needed all the support they could get. Much to my mother's chagrin, she would take the little food they had, put it into what seemed to be magical pots, and turn it into enough food to feed many in a growing line of neighborhood children. One of them went on to be the prime minister of St. Kitts. While we recognize this man's leadership, we often forget my grandmother's role and the leadership she demonstrated. Recognizing and identifying uncelebrated leaders who do the heavy lifting without benefiting from systems is so important. When you provide these folks with paid opportunities to lead, the impact they can have is limitless.

I have been doing work around food for a long time, learning about and interrogating the modern food system and its history—a system founded on stolen land and farmed by stolen people. Indigenous sovereignty and Black liberation are inextricably linked; the issues we face are intertwined, and the opportunities that exist for our communities are intertwined. The first step to building solidarity or effective partnership is to reject transactional relationship building. We need relational interactions, to take the time to sit and get to know our partners. Building partnerships requires entering conversations without an agenda, and rather than action items, you allow space to connect. It can also be detrimental for an organization to be overly focused on, or recognized by, a single leader. In building healthy organizations that can withstand change, we can't be dependent on a charismatic leader with vision. During my time at FoodShare, the organization saw a lot of media coverage. We had grown our budget, become more established, and invested in building new relationships and partnerships. Before I left, we began work internally to recognize team members who could speak with the media and developed an internal speaker bureau. We were building internal capacity.

At Evenings & Weekends, I'm the co-CEO with my cofounder, Laëtitia Eyssartel. She and I had worked together at Foodshare, where she was a senior director. As the name suggests, we had planned to make Evenings & Weekends a side project, something that spoke to our passion for advancing good work in other organizations through collaboration. The biggest asset we have is our team. These are not your typical folks who come into charities to advise on things they've never done themselves. Our team has all worked at charities, leading them through transitions and change. I'm incredibly proud of the team we've created and the quick impact we're already having. We've also found some organizations are not ready for this kind of work and expertise. If they're looking for a quick fix, a checklist to follow, or simple training, then we turn that work down. We all have limited energy, and our work's core mission is to center joy. We talk about that in our meetings—creating more space for work that brings joy. We are not only in business to make money; what drives us is our impact. We are trying to remind people that knowledge exists in many areas and within many people—not just those society tells us are the knowledge holders. Our work is more than consulting; it's about advancing good change. My advice for aspiring leaders is to be curious. Ask why. Why do we do the things we do? Could we do things differently? We have been convinced that many things are inevitable when they are not. Systems can be redesigned.

17

An Ear for Leadership

Zach Phillips *serves as the director of professional development for NAMM, the National Association of Music Merchants. A musician and passionate educator, Zach oversees all educational programming at NAMM. Scott has spoken on three NAMM stages and attended the conference four or five times, several with our older kids. In our experience, conferences or trade shows of NAMM's size often become bigger than themselves and forget about people—but NAMM is different, with a focus on attendees, vendors, and staff—and Zach is a big part of making that happen.*
(Highlights from our interview, recorded June 2, 2023.)

As AN EDUCATIONAL PROGRAMMER, IT'S easy to fall into the mindset of providing what you think people need to be learning about. At NAMM, our strategy is to evaluate the wants of our membership and provide education programs based on those wants; we're totally focused on relevance. We track attendance trends and take feedback from members when evaluating education programs. We're always on the lookout for talent, new topics, and educators who are best suited for our membership. The growing needs of our members and our ability to meet them requires long-term planning, even beyond the next NAMM show. Many of the newer communities we're serving benefit from hands-on education, which is somewhat new to us. For instance, when you're talking about a pro audio attendee, maybe a live sound engineer, they want to get their hands on the gear. They want to try the latest live sound mixing consoles and be educated in the technology behind it. Music technology in general is a big area of growth in our industry, and we have some great partners who provide education on that. We're always looking forward, and tech has become an important part of the ecosystem.

Finding the right partner who can speak the language and the culture of that particular industry vertical is critical. Partnerships are vital to our work because they have expertise in their professional communities that we could never have. We have made it a strategic decision to find associations and media partners that are experts in their field and then work to expand the education they offer. We work to find groups with understanding and influence in their segment. We host an enormous education conference and show with more than 200 sessions, held alongside an exhibit of the most exciting music industry–related products in the world. Our job is to provide guidance when needed and help adapt what they do to the NAMM format because what we do is quite different within the industry.

When COVID hit, we had to cancel one NAMM show and then postpone the next. We knew that like us, our members were facing new challenges and looking for support and resources. Our goal is always to help our members, and so we worked through the spring and summer to formulate a new kind of virtual event, Believe in Music Week. It was a huge success, with 96,000 people attending, which our platform vendor told us was the largest virtual event of any of their clients in terms of total attendance. The energy, enthusiasm, and passion for that event was contagious. During uncertainty, the best leaders are those who are realistic about the challenges before them. They don't put their heads in the sand; they remain focused on the goal and open to creative ways of getting there.

One interesting part of creating Believe in Music Week was that we faced a decision between doing nothing and doing something. The event was intentionally a cost center, not a revenue source, because we believed it was vital to serve our industry during a difficult time. Organizing the event created a moment when mid-level management at NAMM elevated themselves; we had to think differently. We were more reliant on people like our video director, our platform manager, and our web team to move into advisory positions. We were tapping into reserves and resources that hadn't been fully utilized in the organization. Leadership has to come from all levels of your organization.

I've been with NAMM for over ten years and came from one of our industry trade magazines called *Music Inc.*, which differentiated itself by focusing on education. I'm blessed with intellectual curiosity; I'm a big, big reader. The longer I work in a leadership position, the more humbling it becomes. I am challenged every day by the good people I work with. To me, a leader is someone who inspires action, and I'm always looking for opportunities for my team, which require mindfulness and intention. Great leaders strive to see what's happening around them clearly and with good judgment. The challenge is, this requires self-understanding first, an understanding of your own strengths and weaknesses, and a lot of mindfulness. I believe it will be vital for future leaders to develop a mindset of self-understanding because you will be challenged, and you'll be challenged often. You'll be challenged on days you weren't expecting it.

18

Leading with Our Best Friends

Julie Castle is CEO at Best Friends Animal Society, a leading national animal welfare organization dedicated to ending the killing of dogs and cats in America's shelters. A leader in the no-kill movement, Best Friends runs the nation's largest no-kill sanctuary for companion animals, as well as lifesaving programs in collaboration with a nationwide network of members and partners working to save them all. Alison and our 17-year-old Tess have visited Best Friends as volunteers twice, first as a 13th birthday gift and again in March 2019. Funny enough, without knowing our family connection to Best Friends, they also brought Scott in to keynote the 2022 Best Friends National Conference.

(Highlights from our interview, recorded July 18, 2023.)

I'M JULIE CASTLE, THE CEO at Best Friends Animal Society. My journey started in 1994, on a road trip to Mexico that I took with some friends in my beat-up 1979 Dodge Colt. The car was classic, with each panel a different color, representing all of my fender benders. We decided to stay in Mexico until we ran out of money. Puerto Vallarta was our last hurrah before I was due to head to the University of Virginia School of Law.

When we finally ran out of money, with just enough cash to pay for gas and for all of us to have a candy bar each, we embarked on the 1,800-mile trip back to Utah. We were grumpy, hungry, and hadn't showered for days when one of my friends, despite a lot of complaining and whining, convinced us to stop by some out-of-the-way animal sanctuary in a remote area of southern Utah. She wanted to visit a dog who she was sponsoring at this place called Best Friends Animal Sanctuary.

And this is where my life changed in an instant.

The very moment we drove into Angel Canyon and saw the Sanctuary, I was overcome with emotion at the sheer magnitude of the sweeping salmon-colored rocks making up the canyon walls, the rolling hills of red sand that flowed so effortlessly around and under each and every rock, green trees for miles, and skies that were the most vivid shade of blue I had ever seen. It was nothing short of magical.

We walked into the Welcome Center and, given our shabby appearance, were greeted with a wary eye, but still were offered a free tour of the sprawling sanctuary, which was spread out over 3,000 acres of some of the most beautiful land on earth. One of the founders, Judah Battista, drove us around in an old GMC Jimmy that was only a notch more presentable than my Dodge Colt. I peppered him with questions. "Why is this different from a local shelter? What is your philosophy? What is no-kill?" We had lunch with the rest of the founders and volunteers, and I knew this was what I wanted to do. I recalled these words from a book called *The Alchemist* that I read while in Mexico: "The essential wisdom of listening to our hearts, learning to read the omens strewn along life's path, and, above all, following our dreams." And I realized, this is my dream. When we pulled out of the sanctuary, we stopped at a local gas station, I dropped a couple of quarters into a pay phone, and called my dad to break the news that I was not going to law school. I was moving to Kanab to work at an animal sanctuary. Needless to say, he was not pleased. Actually, he flipped out. Everybody in my orbit flipped out. The rest is history.

I moved to Kanab and lived in a van and showered at the gym until I could find a place to live. I became "employee #17." There was no job description—we just did whatever was needed that day: animal care, landscaping, tour guide, whatever. My first paycheck came to $183. It was most definitely a work of the heart. Work at the sanctuary was all hands on deck. I'd show up and get my daily assignment. There was no HR department, and everything was on-the-job training. You didn't have a job description; you just had to figure things out together. If a vehicle needed repair, a broken fence needed mending, or a sprinkler system needed installation, you relied on the local hardware store and Time-Life Books to figure it out.

The gritty, scrappy, can-do attitude of the founders permeated the sanctuary and was one of my greatest life lessons. Things aren't just handed to you, and creating change requires hard work, ingenuity, and both cooperation and self-reliance.

The vision of the founders of Best Friends went way beyond the confines of a beautiful sanctuary. It was to change the way people relate to animals and in particular, the way that animals in shelters are treated. The killing of dogs and cats in America's shelters had to stop.

Animal sheltering began in this country in the 1800s. In big cities like New York, there was a rabies outbreak among the huge street dog population running around the streets, and the public was rightfully concerned. The city put a bounty on the animals, which were rounded up and drowned in public view in the East River at a place that was dubbed the "Dog's Bathtub."

There was a public outcry against this cruelty, and shelters were built to hold the dogs briefly for reclaiming by their owners before being killed behind closed doors. With only minor changes, that's the way the system of animal sheltering remained until the no-kill movement challenged the status quo.

When the founders started the sanctuary, they asked a simple question: "Why aren't we working to save our best friends rather than killing them?" From day one, Best Friends practiced and advocated a no-kill philosophy and quickly became the national voice of the movement. Ending shelter killing nationwide was their vision, but they didn't yet have an on-the-ground strategy. In 2000 I was part of the leadership team that launched No More Homeless Pets in Utah as the first statewide no-kill campaign, which became the template for our national work. We began by looking at data for the state of Utah, which meant getting every shelter's animal data. How many animals were coming in? How many were left alive?

Very basic at first, just cats and dogs. But gradually very sophisticated data analysis became the prevailing model for shelters everywhere.

The founders had built a culture of inclusion. It didn't matter who you loved or what religion you were. If you raised a hand to help, you were welcome. This wasn't a marketing strategy or with any motive other than to help animals. They recognized human beings wanted to feel included and appreciated and wanted to express and share in the gratitude that comes with working to save the lives of animals. As we grew as a value-based organization, doing the right thing couldn't just be an oral tradition—we had to be intentional about how we treat employees, volunteers, and partners.

When I started at Best Friends, I traveled with the founders to different communities, setting up card tables with photos of sanctuary animals and a coffee can for donations to support the sanctuary while building our mailing list. At the end of each day, we'd call home with our results, and the sanctuary team would prioritize which bills to pay first. We'd fax in the names and addresses of people that we met at tables to Angel Canyon. They would enter the names into our growing database and then distribute them to a team of founders who made follow-up calls to thank people and request pledges for future donations. The whole thing was grassroots.

To this day, I meet donors and volunteers in the Village Cafe who remember me from those days. They remember meeting us at some table in Los Angeles or Salt Lake or Santa Fe and being called with a thank-you for even the smallest donations. It is crucial to remember that every single donation is important and to express gratitude for it. Give people the opportunity to take center stage, promote them, and give public recognition. Your responsibility as a leader is to help others grow, see their path forward, and show gratitude.

In late 2009, I was diagnosed with advanced-stage cancer. It was very aggressive, and very scary. I went to UCLA for treatment. It is one of the premiere cancer treatment centers in the world. I was only 39; my chance of survival was up in the air. This was another watershed moment in my personal life and in my career in animal welfare. I thought to myself, "I can sit here and think about how scary this is, or I can get to work and make the most out of my life and go big for the animals." There was a spay-neuter conference in Los Angeles, and I was a panelist. I thought about the city: 400 square miles, six city shelters, 25% of people living under the poverty line. It is one of the largest cities in the world, one of the largest economies in the world. LA Animal Services was taking in 57,000 animals a year and killing 23,000 of them—in the city of hopes and dreams and glitter.

By this time, I was the director of Community Programs and Services at Best Friends, and Los Angeles home to one of our largest membership bases. We had been operating programs there since the early 1990s but had yet to take on the challenge of ending shelter killing in the city, which had a notoriously dysfunctional shelter system. Armed with a go-for-broke attitude and my real-world experience at No More Homeless Pets in Utah, I decided to announce that we would take LA to no-kill. It was a big moment and would require purposefully marshaling the organization's resources and relationships outside the sanctuary.

Fortunately, there was a new general manager at LA Animal Services, Brenda Barnette, who was equally committed to ending shelter killing in LA. Brenda was the partner we needed, and we were the only partner with the know-how, experience, and resources to do the job . . . but first I needed to convince the local stakeholders that this wasn't another worthless committee. We were coming together to create a strategy. Their voices would be baked into the plan, and it would be done based on data, transparency, and accountability. We identified a core group of local leaders, and I met with each of them to lay the groundwork for what would become a coalition of over 150 organizations.

Los Angeles became our launching pad and laboratory for a national no-kill campaign. For example, of those 23,000 animals killed in LA, 7,000 were kittens. Kittens are vulnerable and don't survive well in a shelter environment, so we came up with the idea of creating a large-scale neonatal kitten nursery, and it worked, reducing by almost a third the number of animals being killed. It wasn't just a pipe dream or a bumper sticker. Following a year of coalition building and drilling down on data to the zip code level— there are a lot of zip codes in LA!—Best Friends' NKLA (No-Kill Los Angeles) Initiative launched in early 2012 with the city at a meager 57% annual save rate of shelter animals. By 2020, thanks to the NKLA coalition and committed shelter staff, the city crossed the no-kill threshold save rate of 90%, becoming, at the time, the largest no-kill community in the country. At our 2016 National Conference in Salt Lake City, I jumped out of the box again, by declaring in my keynote address that Best Friends would lead the entire country to no-kill by 2025. It was an audacious goal that I likened to JFK's Moonshot speech. We would need new ideas, new technology, and a total commitment. When I made that speech, only 22% of America's shelters were no-kill—at or above a 90% save rate. Today, over 57% of US shelters and more importantly,

75% of all shelters are at or above a 75% save rate. We are closing in on no-kill 2025.

When I drove into Angel Canyon that fateful day in 1994, an unwashed, grumpy young woman, I could never have imagined where that detour on the road home from Mexico would take me or the adventures that lay ahead.

19

Leadership When Push Comes to Shove

Allison Venditti is the founder of Moms at Work, Canada's largest organ-ization representing working mothers. She is a Career Coach & Human Resources Expert with over 15 years of experience creating programs, policy and change for companies and individuals. She is a fierce advocate, thought leader, and a champion for her community.
(Highlights from our interview, recorded June 22, 2023.)

BEFORE LEAVING CORPORATE AND FOUNDING Moms at Work, my expertise was in HR and disability management. At 33, I suffered a brain injury and spent two years away in recovery. When I was ready to return, the company wrote me off. They literally wrote me a letter telling me I was unemployable, always a great motivator for someone like me. I began coaching, and most of my clients ended up being moms; I had little kids, they had little kids—we just got each other. As my clients grew, I realized they needed each other more than my coaching; they needed a network. I wanted to make a broader change, to create more than a company or industry-based group. No matter where you work or your title, you belong with us. My goal is to help everyone make more money, get a better job, and build a professional community. At Moms at Work, we guarantee we're supporting you, helping to change companies, and working systematically to make legislative changes.

Creating a network takes a lot of time. Our collective is currently capped at 350 people, including many non-moms. I stopped new membership to ensure we kept the community tight and am figuring out the next step. Our programs are full, which is great—but also, our programs are full, so we need more. Holding that boundary is hard, but we teach others to do the same. Saying no to growth lets me devote 30% of everything we do to advocacy. I've dedicated the last decade to fighting for pay transparency, and it's working. I started my career in unions, and as an HR person, I put up job postings with the wage included. We had a wage grid; you could open your collective agreement and know what everybody in the organization made. When I began HR in a private company, they asked, "How much do you want to make?" That made no sense to me! I challenged the policy and was told, "That's just how it's done." Who says, right? That's the question. If I put up a job posting for 12 bucks an hour and you need to make 24, why don't we save everyone the time and energy?

There was a shift as women entered the workforce; people stopped openly discussing pay. We've been fighting to close the wage gap for decades, and even when legislation is in place, it has no teeth; women are often fired after formal complaints and salary reviews. Pay transparency is simple; every HR person knows how much that job pays. No company puts out a job posting if they don't have a budget attached to it. Being transparent saves time; not being transparent disrespects the job hunter. Pay transparency is simple as a piece of legislation; put pay on the job posting, and don't ask people what they're currently making because that's used to underpay. We've created a pay transparency tool kit to provide statistics and tips for discussing it at work. It won't solve all equity issues, but paying everyone fairly is a good place to start.

People are leaning toward companies that show up and stand for things. If you cannot afford to pay your people well, you are not a legitimate company. You need to step aside.

In 2020, Moms at Work did Canada's first survey on women's experiences during parental leave. Shockingly, or not so shockingly, 4 in 10 women considered quitting during the return-to-work process. Three out of 10 said they were openly discriminated against for being pregnant or having children, and 95% said they received no support during that transition. Parental leave is my area of expertise, so we went to work. We took the top 150 questions women had and turned them into a free program called My Parental Leave. We talk about more than just the basics, topics like pregnancy and infant loss, postpartum depression, and tax implications. Knowledge is power. With the kit, women can go confidently to their employers and speak about what's legal and what's not.

COVID brought new challenges. I've been in HR for a long time, and I knew things would be bad for women and mothers specifically, and I wasn't wrong. I'm not going to lie; there have been so many times when I cried under my desk, watching my community fall apart; women who worked 20 years left their jobs to care for sick loved ones. And it is not over; these people's careers were decimated. People are acting like it's over, but it isn't. You can't forget how you were treated, because when push came to shove, you were shoved. Many struggle during phases of life like parenting and carry on, leaving others behind them to suffer. Having a baby or young children and fighting for rights at work is exhausting. Most of us are too tired—but I'm not. The only way to make change is to show up. It can be overwhelming when there are so many problems; pick one and get to work.

20

A Note on Hiring

IN THE AGE OF DISRUPTION, your talent strategy is a marketing tool, from job description to interview. Hiring happens in public, and your language and processes shape your brand reputation and ability to attract the talent you need. Depending on where you operate, legal, compliance, and regulatory considerations, including pay transparency, must be considered (as Allison Venditti just advocated for so brilliantly). Attracting a diverse workforce requires considering your biases and the candidates you want to reach.

Inclusive language in job postings is a key factor in reducing bias. Leaders should be mindful of gendered job titles, such as "businessman" or "salesman," and avoid stereotypes and gender-coded language, removing "he, she, his, and hers" pronouns and coded terms like "assertive, aggressive, or ambitious," which can deter women and gender-diverse applicants. Racial and cultural bias are also evident in terms like "native English speaker," or postings that require education from a particular institution or at a level beyond the role's requirements. Not everyone has the same access to educational opportunities, and this type of language devalues past work experience and schools beyond the Ivy League. Age-related terms like "young and energetic" or "digitally native" are limiting, and requiring "no more than X years of experience" only serves to discriminate against older, more experienced workers.

To get you started on considering bias in your job postings, several tools are available online to help with your hiring. The Gender Decoder[1] is an online tool inspired by research from Danielle Gaucher, Justin Friesen, and Aaron C. Kay, which showed women are less likely to apply to job listings that include masculine-coded language. The site allows you to plug in your ad and check for language shown to limit responses.

The Conscious Style Guide[2] offers help to writers and editors who want to think critically about language, including "words, portrayals, framing, and representation—to empower instead of limit." The site is a rich resource, offering guides and articles to study words so that "they can become tools instead of unwitting weapons." The founder, Karen Yin encourages writers (and yes, a job posting is writing) to question their assumptions about their audience and consider language's potential impact. We recommend checking out the comprehensive guides, which include topics around design and images, ethnicity, race and nationality, teaching and other educational settings for children, age, ability, gender, sex and sexuality, appearance, climate, and the environment.

Far too many companies rely on recycled, outdated job postings and descriptions. Inclusive language does more than ensure the best people apply for your position; it also signals to the workforce that you value diversity and inclusion. A job posting is often the first experience an applicant has with a company or brand, and it can be the beginning of fostering inclusion. Leaders should be upfront, clear, and concise about what they offer, from pay to work

---

[1] https://gender-decoder.katmatfield.com.
[2] https://consciousstyleguide.com.

hours, requirements, accommodations, and other benefits. Use precise language, limit jargon, and seek experts to help uncover biases limiting your company's talent. The days when all the power in hiring belonged to the employer are over; your job postings need to anticipate concerns and share why a candidate should want to join your team.

21

Leading by Example

Derek Jones is director of community relations at Buffini & Company, a business coaching and training company based in San Diego. He joined Buffini & Company in 2007 and since that time has served in a variety of roles, working with the company's Buffini Group Leaders, managing the company's world-class events, and growing the organization's vast network of clients, all of which has brought him face-to-face with thousands of clients and customers.

(Highlights from our interview, recorded May 22, 2023.)

I PLAYED BASKETBALL IN HIGH school and college, and you always knew who the team captain would be. They presented themselves long before they were officially chosen by the coach. They wouldn't always be the best players—they would be the people who worked the hardest. The person the team gravitated to, who was present, dedicated, and checking in on their teammates. Leadership by example is a philosophy that has always stuck with me and guided my work, whether as a sales manager or running our events. Leadership isn't something you arrive at; it's constant. You have to be changing. Otherwise, it's easy to become trapped in a role. Being a disruptor once doesn't make you a leader forever. You have to keep your finger on the needs of the people you serve and stay connected and informed.

The power of delegation has been a huge leadership lesson for me since beginning at Buffini & Company, and it's one I still struggle with. Typically, you become a leader because you were a great doer, right? You were the person in the trenches doing the work and were given recognition. Then a position opens up in management or something, and now you're leading the team—in charge of doing that thing. But there is a gap; no one teaches you how to lead. For a leader, delegation is important because it frees you up to do other things—to motivate the team and bring the whole project forward. I'm thankful to work in an environment where it's OK to ask questions and say you aren't sure what you're doing in a particular situation. The best leaders take the time to be humble and admit when they have a problem. You have to be ready to ask and ready to learn.

When too focused on the doing, we miss out on creative ways to reach our goal. I don't have a tattoo, but if I did, it would say, "What are we trying to accomplish?" Anytime someone on my team comes to me with a challenge, that's where we start. Then we work together to figure things out. This keeps us moving forward as a team in a constructive way and helps with conflict resolution, something that translates outside a work environment. When implementing a project and working to get people on board, I give as much context as possible. This means understanding the impact and communicating the intent behind what we're trying to do. Understanding context also allows your team to come up with creative ideas. As a leader, I share context and intent and encourage my team to decide how we get there.

I want new members to know our history and feel their voice is important to moving us forward into the future. I want our aspiring leaders to understand their value and that everyone brings something to the table. Empowerment is key. A healthy company has an environment where everybody can lead from wherever they're at, but that environment has to be created, and you have to be intentional to do that. The front line shouldn't need to justify their value. They grow into the next round of leaders. You have to be intentional about connection and communication. A lot of companies take connections for granted just because everyone is in the same space, but that's not necessarily true. It's too easy to blame the pandemic and say, "Oh my gosh, we're losing this connection because everyone's at home." Not really; it's just that the connection wasn't as strong as you thought. Everyone was in the same room, so you assumed you didn't have to think about it—but you do. We are relational beings. Being connected to other people is in our DNA. It's evolutionarily and what keeps us going. The more we connect with others, the better our lives will be.

22

Unorthodox Leadership

Back in 2014, when we wrote UnSelling, valuing people was at the heart of our message. Treating employees, vendors, and customers well is the start of creating amazing experiences and standing out in today's busy world of information and reviews. We spoke about hiring for passion, creating quality products first, and then service and content worth sharing. We wanted companies to make it easy for fans to tell your brand story for you and facilitate community around your product and/or service. That is the way to create an ecstatic customer base; that's UnSelling. One of our favorite case studies was Big Ass Fans, an American company that manufactures fans, evaporative coolers, and controls for industrial, agricultural, commercial, and residential use. What first caught our attention was an article about how the company paid their employees 30% above the national median and 50% above Kentucky's median, where they were located. We reached out to their CEO, Carey Smith, who shared how their no layoffs policy had saved thousands in recruiting costs and training new employees and that Big Ass Fans also offered education scholarships and valued employee satisfaction and well-being.[1]

---

[1] Carey shared a ton of awesome advice! To read more of it, see our book *UnSelling: The New Customer Experience* (Hoboken, New Jersey: Wiley, 2014).

Speaking with Carey almost 10 years later for UnLeadership, we found him in a new role as CEO of investment firm Unorthodox Ventures. Here are some of the highlights of our interview.

(Highlights from our interview, recorded July 19, 2023.)

I'm CAREY SMITH, CEO (OR founding contrarian, as I prefer) of investment firm Unorthodox Ventures. Before that, I was the CEO (or chief big ass) at Big Ass Fans, a company I founded in 1999 and sold in 2017. The $500 million sale of the fan and light company came about because I needed a change. It wasn't because it had been the plan all along. Running a venture capital firm, you meet many people who start businesses with one goal in mind: to sell and make a lot of money at exit. At Big Ass Fans, we weren't in business to make money. We made money to stay in business.

Starting out, I didn't have any money, so I bootstrapped the operation, with my wife kindly agreeing to sell our house and then cosigning every credit card offer that showed up in our mailbox. And I mean every credit card. We had dozens and maxed out each of them. That may sound risky, but it meant we didn't have to keep any investors happy. I was able to make decisions focused on the long-term future and not just the bottom line. When you use your own money, you don't have a fiduciary responsibility to others; you lead as you see fit, and Big Ass Fans grew into a recognizable brand in large part because it expressed how I looked at life and business.

We always spent lavishly on customer service, because your customers are the best advertisement (our net promoter score tripled the industry average), and it's the right thing to do to stand behind the product you make. While it may cost more, you'll make more revenue in the long term because customers become repeat customers. By the time I sold the company, our customer loyalty was so strong that repeat business accounted for half of all orders, even as our number of new customers increased 40% annually. We spent just as handsomely on our employees. We paid them 50% higher than the state average and 30% more than the national average. We also offered them challenging, interesting, exciting work, so it's no wonder our employee retention rate exceeded 90%, while the rest of the country hovers in the 50% to 60% range.

Employees appreciate you more and are willing to work harder when you spend money on them. Imagine that! I learned that lesson early. Growing up, my mother worked as a secretary. She would often receive a turkey as a Christmas bonus, and it drove her up the wall. Even as a child, I took this in and realized the bonus cost the company nothing. Giving her $15 would have been more helpful; a few hundred dollars would have shown they were thinking of her, empathizing with her position and appreciating her. At Big Ass Fans, I made sure employees felt appreciated, at Christmas and all year round, and that generosity helped us solve problems that frustrate the average company. For example, getting a large group of people to come in at the same time every day is difficult; they are supposed to be there at 8, but some arrive at 7:45 and others at 8:15. Many companies react punitively in these situations, but we decided to reward those who arrived within 5 minutes consistently with a dollar an hour increase in pay. And at the end of the month, everyone in the group was treated to a big lunch with lots of leftovers to take home and share with their families. We solved the problem, as 90% of our employees arrived on time. It cost a little money, sure, but it saved so much more because our operations ran smoothly and on time. When you have a problem, approach it positively, empathize with those doing the work, and actually take the time to ask them for their thoughts. That way, everybody wins.

Leaders lead by thinking long-term. Everybody can see what's right in front of them; a leader has to be able to convince people that they see beyond the horizon. This doesn't mean every leader has to be a once-in-a-century visionary. I simply got up early, went to bed late, and thought about the business 24/7. Leaders should be able to express goals to others and ensure the group sees how each person contributes to that goal and how it helps everyone when we succeed. People are more likely to buy into ideas when they understand why a plan is viable. When you have employees' attention, you can lead them anywhere. Without it, people see their jobs (and themselves) as just a number.

If your company seems chaotic at times, know that leadership often emerges from a mess. We once opened an office in Australia after having learned how terrible it was to try to sell through distributors, who push every product including your competitors' and will never know the differences between any of them. Most of our staff was young and had yet to be west of the Mississippi River, but we knew we needed our own people there to see things through. I went to them and said, "Hey, I want you to move to Australia for three years and start the office. We have nothing there, so you have to organize the whole thing; find a facility, do all the hiring, figure out the logistics, and do all the marketing." The people who stepped up for that project became leaders because they had to figure things out independently.

That is the difference between a supervisor, a manager, and a leader. A supervisor tells people what to do and leaves. A manager is responsible for telling you what to do and ensuring it gets done and continues. A leader uses a holistic approach, recognizing the team's strengths and weaknesses, and then offers support. A leader transcends the situation and looks to the future. A real leader stands up and says, "I've thought about this, and this is what we ought to do."

23

Leading with Content

BACK IN 2009 (OMG), WHEN we wrote *UnMarketing*, social media, content creation, and influencer marketing were the disruptive topics of the day. Over the years, we have shared best practices for audio, video, and written content and countless how-tos of creation and curation. As leaders, we can become overwhelmed by all the methods of information delivery available and forget the most critical point—no matter the platform, it is the content itself that matters most. If you do not have great content, it does not matter at all how you deliver it.

So, you may be asking, what makes content great? Well, as always it comes back to relationships; those you build with your team, your market, and your intended audience. Content is shared because it evokes emotion, good or bad. To go viral, your content has to reach and travel with your "third circle": those without a previous close relationship to you. For example, if Alison shares a video of our dog Chelsea on a walk, Scott would 100% like and maybe even share that photo. But if Chelsea was also dressed for the

Barbie movie,[1] more people would share it, even if they didn't know us or Chelsea; emotion sticks and travels.

To learn more about content and content creation we spoke to expert **Jon Youshaei**. *He is one of a few marketers to work at both YouTube and Instagram and has been featured in* Business Insider, Time, *and* Inc Magazine *for "cracking the code to going viral." During five years at YouTube, Jon was head of Creator Product Marketing, where he worked with YouTube's top creators and brands to grow their audience and their incomes. During three years at Instagram, Jon helped build their creator team to empower even more creators to grow and monetize. Now a creator himself, Jon has garnered 500K+ followers and 300M+ views working with brands such as Google, Hubspot, and Fiverr. Jon is also a sought-after speaker, advisor, and investor whose focus is on putting out content that educates creators on how to build successful businesses online.*

(Highlights from our interview, recorded June 20, 2023.)

Right now is one of the best times to be a creator. More specifically, there's a lot of opportunity for creators with professional experience who can share their expertise on camera and actively research, find inspiration, experiment, and adapt. It reminds me of a Mark Twain quote: "There is no such thing as a new idea. It is impossible. We simply take a lot of old ideas and put them into a sort of mental kaleidoscope. We give them a turn and they make new and curious combinations." Simply put, you're either aware or unaware of that inspiration—you can be deliberate, trying to get as much input and inspiration as possible, or you ignore it, and your output is always going to be worse.

Anything I teach, I experiment with first. Things that work today may be quickly outdated, so we have to keep our skills as sharp as possible. Taking what I learned at companies like YouTube, and combining that with having free rein to experiment, is part of the

---

[1] Hi Barbie!

reason we've grown so much in our first year. Experimentation and putting what we've learned into practice lets us grow in confidence and advise the folks we work with. Right now, people are obsessed with short-form content: YouTube Shorts, TikTok, Instagram Reels, and Snapchat, etc. But the real question is, how can you make sure that trend helps you grow a business, makes people remember who you are and what you're about? You need to figure out how short-form content leads to long form, and actual results. People are so fixated on short forms, they forget the multiformat nature of content. Communication style is also very important, simplifying speech without dumbing it down. Choose words that accurately capture what you want to say, and focus on the audience and why they're there. Think about being succinct, without losing the message and who you are.

When I have an idea for a cartoon, for example, I take my sketch and share it with folks to get as much feedback as possible and see how the idea resonates. If I'm making content for a specific audience, like creators, I talk to aspiring creators, emerging creators, and established creators across the spectrum. If I am creating something for a broader appeal, I show it to different people; I've shown videos to my Uber driver. I'll show it to my dad and mom. English isn't their first language, but they understand what I'm trying to do. If I'm speaking too fast, or the content gets too niche too quickly, they'll help me balance my message. Putting your work out there and getting feedback is something I saw the benefits of early on. It's also just more fun. That's why my podcast is called *Created with Jon Youshaei*—I love creating with other folks.

My advice to aspiring leaders in the creator space is to start experimenting before you go all in. Many people believe they have to throw caution to the wind, but I am a big believer in figuring out what you can do to limit risk as much as possible. Find ways to get better on camera, better at writing, and practice doing all the things that make up a career as a creator. There are two factors that go into making content interesting—experience and entertainment—and the holy grail is making your expertise entertaining. A lot of people turn on the camera and try to be entertaining, but that takes a lot of talent. With experience and expertise, you've won half the battle; now you have to figure out the hook. How can I make this entertaining? What examples can I use to make the expertise relatable? You can de-risk by focusing on practice and getting as much expertise as possible.

When I was younger, I thought people were anointed as a mentor, but it's never that formal. Everything is fluid, and different people give different pieces of advice in different moments of your life, and then you can return the favor. Even if you're young, you can do that.

For me, one of the biggest blessings has been my wife becoming my business manager. She previously worked in corporate settings and operations and has brought a level of professionalism to my work. Leadership is really about partnerships, and I would never be able to do all this without my wife, her help, and our partnership.

24

A Note on Mentorship

MANY EXPERTS WILL TELL YOU that if you want to build success in business, find a mentor. It makes a lot of sense. We leave school, join the workforce, and kind of have to figure things out on our own from there. Mentorship at its best offers advice, experience, and the opportunity to ask questions of someone more knowledgeable about a certain field. Especially in a context where asking questions is viewed as risky or denotes ignorance, mentorship can be a safe space to learn and grow.

Going into our interviews, we assumed almost every leader would have a mentor, but we were wrong. A few issues arose. Mentorship, like anything, means different things to different people. Traditional mentorship within corporations doesn't always consider the value newer workers bring to the table, often around critical things like innovation and technology. Mentorship doesn't guarantee access to resources or opportunities for further networking. A mentor may or may not share their network and resources with a mentee—and often this is what they need more than anything else. Also, traditionally mentors are held up on a pedestal as "the example," when really, they are just one example. Today's leaders need more than one person to emulate—they need to gather stories, build networks, and find support in many different areas.

In *UnSelling* we wrote a chapter called "Beware of Mountain Climbers Who Sell Equipment." Picture a successful mountain climber standing on the summit, exhausted, exhilarated. With their success comes people who want to learn about the climbers' strategy. What equipment did they use? How did they pace the ascent? The so-called best practices we look for in business. What if this climber, instead of listing off all the equipment and strategies, threw all of the stuff off the other side of the mountain and said you don't need anything at all—except my new book/course/consulting on "How to Climb to the Summit of Success." Even if they aren't quite that malicious and they share all their equipment and strategies, they're still up there on the mountain, and you're trying to make your way up alone. And, over time, they'll forget all the struggle, fear, and risk—so even if they remember the tools, the emotions are forgotten. There is no such thing as an easy trip to the top, without hard work, luck, support, and a whole lot of tools.

The view is different from the top of the mountain. Your connections are different, your credibility is different, and the size of your platform is different. We love retrospective advice, where we look back and share how "we would have climbed the mountain differently." But we need to be cautious and start where our teams and mentees are and what tools they are going to need for success. And please, take extra care when the climber on the top of the mountain says the only way up is to buy a tool kit with their name on it, because that's the worst advice of all. All of us have leaders we look up to, who we have learned from and have shaped our experiences. However, to be a leader we need more than one mentor and more than mentorship. As you step into leadership positions and into mentorship, remember there are many pathways to success.

Source: Every Vowel, https://www.everyvowel.com/evcartoon/oxygen-mask//, last accessed 9 October, 2023

25

Leadership Is More Than a Label

Julie Cole is a recovered lawyer, mom of six, and cofounder and senior director of Mabel's Labels. She is an award-winning entrepreneur, best-selling author, and sought-after speaker, moderator, keynote, and emcee. When not juggling her busy family and professional life, Julie is an engaged community member serving on boards and volunteering. She is passionate about women's issues, mentoring young entrepreneurs, and social justice.
(Highlights from our interview, recorded June 20, 2023.)

WE STARTED MABEL'S LABELS WITH four cofounders: my sister and two friends from university who ended up marrying my brother and young uncle. Having a team was advantageous early on because entrepreneurship can be very lonely. When one of us was having a bad day, or a baby, and wondering what we'd gotten ourselves into, the other three were there to rally, to be cheerleaders and a peer group. Having four different ways of leading is wonderful because there's no perfect style. As we've grown, our roles have changed, and our leadership styles have evolved as we've become more confident. It has always been instinctual; as challenges came up, whoever's skills and personality fit best stepped up and was supported.

Writing business plans on playdates, we were results oriented from the start and wanted to extend this to our company culture. Focusing on results and communication created a strong management culture. We learned we couldn't micromanage. We needed to let people learn and let them go to do their jobs; otherwise, it hurts retention. We didn't want to focus on presenteeism or force employees to be dishonest to make their kids' holiday concerts or doctor's appointments. When COVID hit, many companies scrambled with remote and hybrid work, but we already had systems in place. It was our time to shine. We give our employees the freedom to be entrepreneurial and delight our customers. This makes our staff team happy and makes Mabel's more profitable; it's good for business.

In leadership, you have to get comfortable with being uncomfortable because things are always changing. I compare it to parenting. First, you have babies and get a handle on that, and then all of a sudden, they're preschoolers, and it's a whole different game.

One of the greatest leadership challenges we've faced, especially around transparency, was when Mabel's was acquired by Avery, which is owned by a publicly traded company, CCL. Rules meant that we couldn't discuss the process with our staff or even say we were in negotiations. We had a coach, Liane Davey, help figure out the best way to deliver the news. We ensured there was support, information, and were available to answer any questions or concerns. We gave everyone a gift card for a local coffee shop and told them any of us, at any time, would drop whatever we were doing to go for a sit-down and talk about how they were feeling about the changes. We were so afraid of going to that staff meeting, but it was a success. One of our directors stood up and clapped, and we celebrated together. Spending time with Liane and drafting a clear, concise message that inspired trust was a huge leadership lesson for us. When leading a team through uncertainty, you can't go in unprepared with your hair on fire.

Having a personal brand has always been a part of Mabel's. Our market is moms who want to buy from something other than nameless, faceless brands. Over the years, that personal brand has changed. I'm not talking about pushing a triple stroller or explosive diapers anymore because I'm not that mom today. Now we have our awesome community managers on TikTok with their kids. With every post, every comment, and every speaking engagement, you are making a brand impression, and you have to be extremely mindful of that. Recently we made inclusive pronoun labels and had some angry customers who felt we'd gone too far and told us they wouldn't be buying from us anymore. And you know what, we were OK with that. Our core values are about accepting and respecting individuals, and we stand by that. We train our community managers to understand the brand's voice and message. On the flip side, if I define myself as the cofounder of Mabel's Labels, I might have an identity crisis when I'm not there anymore; personal brand is important, but you can't hold on to it too long. Twenty years into this entrepreneurial journey, curating leadership in others and seeing them flourish is what I find most fulfilling. We have to pass the mic, step back, give accolades, and check our ego at the door.

26

Leadership That Outshines

With a distinguished 25-plus-year career of leadership in music, entertainment, social media, and influencer marketing sectors, **Barbara Jones is** *the founder and CEO of Outshine Talent, a talent management company that represents social creators, musicians, college athletes, and innovators.*
(Highlights from our interview, recorded July 7, 2023.)

I'M PASSIONATE ABOUT CREATIVE PEOPLE because, honestly, I can't sing, dance, or act; I'm not a front-facing person. I love being behind the scenes and have always been an organizer and a planner. Starting in the music business out of college, I have been lucky to always have a passion-based job. But the higher up on the corporate chain I moved, the less fulfilled I was by the work. In the music business, you can have the best job ever, and then there's a regime change; they clean the house and want to bring in their own people. That's what happened to me, and I had to decide whether to find another job or do something new.

I was intrigued by what was happening with social media, and in the summer of 2007, I heard about the BlogHer conference; it was an aha moment for me. I knew I could return to the music business if things didn't work out. I gave myself a year. Entrepreneurship started for me in middle school. I was always selling something; I've always been resourceful and a bit of a hustler. I knew entertainment people, but they were only in music. I had to get to know the brand people, the agency folks, and a new group who weren't yet called influencers. I was confident I could organize a cool event, so I started with a conference to bring together brands, agencies, and bloggers. As a liaison, I was at the center and leveraged that position to build my blog network/influencer marketing company.

Over the years, convincing others and being an educator, communicator, and liaison between brands and influencers has been a huge part of my job. I built a large database of influencers and worked to help brands match and reach the right audiences. There have always been influencers. Word of mouth isn't a new concept; only the depth and breadth of where information can go has changed. With data, we can now share stories and narratives and prove impact. As a marketer before the Internet, we couldn't always show a direct correlation between narrative, interaction, and conversation. In 1991, I was marketing for Nirvana by passing out stickers on Sunset Boulevard outside shows, you know? People take the measurement for granted now.

As a leader in the space, we're always looking, but we're not always signing. We look for unicorns, the people we feel we can develop. Youth culture is driving everything, so we have to understand what's important and their behaviors and see where the tides are turning. For me, it's instinctual, like my spidey sense. In 2019, I saw what was happening with TikTok; it was palpable. I left the agency and went into creator management. When you surround yourself with smart, forward-thinking people, things come up, and you see opportunities and trends. I love being on the early end of things because there are no rules—you get to make them up as you go. First, it was Facebook, Twitter, YouTube, blogging, then Pinterest and Instagram; now we had to figure out Snapchat and Vine for a moment and then TikTok. With each new thing, I had to learn it, figure out who was important in the space and how to best work with a client who hired me for a particular platform. It was always about community—the community happening in each space. I knew if I could build fans for bands, I could build them for brands.

I don't think there is such a thing as mass media anymore. Instead, there are communities; if you have a community, that's all you need. I've been doing this work for a long time, and every day, I discover someone with millions of followers who I'd never heard of before because they're outside my personal community. There was a time when we only had a few stations, only a few places we could go to collectively to see things, and there were gatekeepers. The beauty of the last 15 years is you can be the queen of your own fiefdom; you don't need a record label, publisher, or major production company. There are so many ways to share your work, and it's all about relationships, community, and the social aspect of social media.

The beauty of this space is that it's born out of youth culture. There is an opportunity for young people to get into this world because they have the audience companies are trying to reach. Don't think yourself too young or green—understand you know the audience and their behaviors. Do you want to work at Apple or with Beyoncé? Just start. It all goes back to relationships and treating others with respect. Practice your communication and writing because being a good communicator is your most valuable skill. Brands need to stop looking at the follower counts and start looking at the creator's relationship with their audience. People forget this is not broadcast media; it's social media. Creators are not performing for an audience per se; it's supposed to be a relationship with their audience. You can have a lot of followers and post a lot of content, but without engagement, there isn't a relationship; no personal feeling leads you to take action when the time is right. Brands that do well look for storytellers, find the right person, and utilize their content for campaigns.

27

Planting Leadership Seeds

Cheyenne Sundance is a greens and squash farmer who sells wholesale in Ontario. Cheyenne started Sundance Harvest, an ecological farm in southwestern Ontario in 2019. With a strong interest in incubators, community land trust and cooperative farming she co-founded Sundance Commons, a non-profit that provides the tools, long-term land access, markets, and training for new farmers historically-excluded from the agricultural sector. Sundance Commons provides all these resources at no cost to new farmers and aligns with the spirit of community land trusts. Aside from farming, Cheyenne likes puppet theatre and dancing at discotheques.
(Highlights from our interview, recorded July 26, 2023.)

I FOUNDED SUNDANCE HARVEST IN 2019, when I was 22. Founding the farm and forging that path has been difficult. The common suggestion was to find a mentor, but no one else was doing exactly what I wanted to do. I had to mentor myself, put together elements of what I needed and put those together. I went to farms that were doing winter greens and asked questions about winter greens, went to friends who were good communicators and asked how to become a better communicator. More recently, I went to Virginia and hung out with my friend Chris Newman, who runs a successful pasture-raised poultry operation. He mentored me on chicken production and helped me make a profit and loss sheet. I had to be realistic and figure out what my demographic wanted, so I went to farmers' markets to see what people were buying and when. That's how I learned; I did market research. I was passionate, but passion is one thing and paying the bills is another—I had to make sure people wanted what I would provide.

I'm also president of one of the three caucuses of the National Farmers Union in Canada, which has roots in Saskatchewan (so lots of wheat). Before me, there was no BIPOC caucus across Canada for the union. I pushed and fought for constitutional change, and it was voted through. The coolest thing about the National Farmers Union is their machinery co-op. With grain, you don't need a combine every single day of the year, maybe only a week or two of the year. They cost a lot, but if you share the cost among 20 people, you can use it when needed and technically rent to own it together. I love independence but don't like working alone—so co-ops are very interesting to me. I know I can't grow everything; I can't do chickens, I can't do flowers, I can't do everything at once. But if I work collectively with everyone, we can sell really well. Right now, I am growing with six other farmers, and then I sell the crops at the farmers' markets. Although Sundance has hired amazing teams in the past, there's so much responsibility having employees in farming because the career is so risky. Everyone's money relies on the crops. You cut through uncertainty with a co-op because everyone has to share it. It isn't Cheyenne who is responsible for everyone's wages; everyone is responsible.

Cooperative farming is the biggest connection piece for me because raising livestock is a hard thing. I can run an acre by myself for vegetables, but chickens need someone there to let them out every morning and night; that's a lot of work. I grow chickens with my friend Yusef, and we work cooperatively so no one gets burned out. We can scale in the future, and he has a skill set I still need, being a carpenter and a handyman, and I bring marketing to the table. In a co-operative environment, relationships aren't transactional; we all provide skills and support to each other. Everyone has a bigger stake in the work because they can own part of the operation, which is more fair.

At Sundance, we are now only expanding through cooperation. If I want someone to work with me, rather than hiring them, I offer them land where they can grow what they like, and we cooperatively sell it. I am also transitioning to 100% wholesale, which has already started and is cool. We have some wholesale contacts to groceries, food banks, and restaurants. I'm learning a whole new side of the business.

I bring a lot of educational components to Sundance Harvest. Diversity, equity, and inclusion training doesn't make sense to me; instead of sitting in a room discussing oppression, why can't I have things that will make the world more equitable? So we learn about fixing tractors, using funds for practical skills because practice is equity. I no longer have an urban farm; I do 100% rural farming. I did a talk for the Walrus[1] a month ago, and they wanted me to talk about urban farming, and I told them urban farming is a mistake, a myth, and a lie. People started laughing, but I wasn't kidding. I see horse farms when I drive around the region, so why are we urban-farming? It is marginal land of poor quality, cannot scale, and costs a huge amount of money. Rural land costs less, even with water and such. Urban farming is great for educating people in the city who want to start a farm and then have them incubate and leave; that is what I did this year; I have six incubators in the city, and they learn and move.

---

[1] https://thewalrus.ca/about/.

I've figured farming out as I go, have been light on my feet and pivoted at least 17 times. People might think I don't have a set purpose or direction, but trying out as much as possible while I'm young is pretty smart. Now, I feel confident and finally steady on my feet. As good as it is to learn from others, it's also important to block out people's advice. If you have low risk, why not try it all? I like starting new farms, running new things, and trying new things. It makes the most sense for me to do that cooperatively because it's lower risk. If someone wants to start their own farm, I help them, and then we sell together. Right now, I'm focusing on planting seeds and watching others do cool things.

28

Serious Leadership

We must admit, we have a soft spot for business partnerships; maybe because we know neither of us could have written this book alone. As part of our research on leadership, we wanted to speak with other partners and see how their leadership journeys have been shaped. For us, leading with a partner is about collaboration and making space for the work each of us enjoys and thrives in the most. Today that means one of us is writing this chapter, while the other is on his way to St. Louis to speak at a conference (lucky St. Louis. . .).

To learn more about leadership and partnership, Alison sat down with **Khara Koffel** *and* **Megan Luckey**, *the co-owners of Serious Lip Balm.*
(Highlights from our interview, recorded July 27, 2023.)

I'm **Khara Koffel.** I'm one of the co-owners of Serious Lip Balm. I am a college art professor and sculptor who inadvertently started a lip balm business with my friend Luckey 10 years ago. It's been a ride ever since.

Picture it, Illinois 2013, and although I never intended on having children, my son Jones Perry Benner was born. It didn't take me long to realize day care center teachers were highly undervalued in our community. Rather than giving them a "Number 1 Teacher" mug for Christmas, I decided these angels deserve something they could use and would love, something handmade. A student of mine, Megan Luckey, loved yarn and was always knitting and crocheting. At the time, arm knitting was popular, and so together we learned how to do it, and I roped her into making arm-knitted scarves for all the day care center teachers. The next fall I was on sabbatical, thinking about what to make the teachers that year, when I thought about lip balm. I had no idea how to make it, but that didn't stop me. I did research, ordered all the materials, and called up Luckey. And that's how the magic began—with teacher gifts in 2014.

We're coming up on 10 years working together. We didn't mean to start the business; we just wanted to help as many people as we could, and it fell into place. There has been a lot of hard work, but we get to stumble and get up again. The time has been a learning process, which is beautiful because it allows you to figure out what's important. Both of us are people who look at something and think, "I could do that." We don't have all the money in the world, so we have to figure things out. That's a good thing and a bad thing, right? Now, we look at our strengths and play to those. We have to decide if something is Khara work, Luckey work, or something we should trust someone else to do.

During the pandemic, we switched our focus to more charitable stuff. Instead of stressing about sales, we raised money and sent lip balms to hospitals. We used our popularity on social media to launch Shop Tiny, where we featured other stores and makers. When you do good things, good things come back. Creativity has definitely been our strength. We don't have backgrounds in business, so we had to be humble and learn. We've always been ourselves in business; our marketing has always been 100% Khara and Luckey, and we've never had to pretend to be anything else.

If you're thinking about starting a business, my advice is to try. Test out your idea; you never know, and you're never going to know how awesome you can be if you don't try. Fail. Make mistakes. You never know the impact you will have on yourself and others. Our partnership is based on a high five—if I have nothing left, I can walk over to her and high-five, and she'll pick it up and vice versa. We have hard conversations and love each other hard. In the end, she's my emergency contact, and I've been married for 15 years. Luckey and I are both very outgoing when we need to be, but at the end of the day we both need to sit in the corner, suck on M&M's, and watch weird shows on Netflix to recharge. I couldn't do these 13-hour days with anyone else.

I'm **Megan Luckey** (everybody calls me Luckey) and I'm one of the co-inventors of Serious Lip Balm. I am a sign language interpreter who was inadvertently roped into starting a company with my college professor while double majoring in art.

I will preface this by saying that my longest relationship is with my dog, but the second longest is with Khara. We work collaboratively, like we share a brain. Over the years we've built trust and have learned to say, "She's got it." I'd say 99% of the time when we go somewhere, Khara has no idea where we're staying or how we're getting anywhere; she just trusts that I do. She is like our little engine that could, and I am the one who says, "Whoa, let's talk a little bit about how we're doing this." We all need engines, and we all need logic. Growing up I learned about leadership from my dad, and I know Khara would say the same. My dad is a strong, personable, corn-fed Midwesterner who knows how to do everything and is always ready to teach with kindness and patience. Khara's dad is like the East Coast version of mine, the Pennsylvania Dutch version of cornbread.

We didn't mean to go into business; I was just making lip balm with my friend. It has been a wild journey, full of figuring things out, tears, and lots of ice cream. The biggest challenge has always been time—finding time and then figuring out how to spend it well. Deciding whether or not to get someone else to do something when I can figure it out myself has always been the hardest part. For example, we had a big catalog last year, and we were both so excited to design it, but we ended up hiring a woman locally who did a beautiful job. It was rewarding to trust someone else with a job we could have done. I think this is a big challenge, especially for people with arts backgrounds. We realized at this point, even though we could do the catalog, it wasn't the best use of our time. My advice for other business owners or people who want to start is, don't pour from an empty bucket. You have to take care of yourself and your mental health. And pack extra UnCrustables on the road.

29

Leadership Is a Compass, Not a Map

*In 1995, **Martin and Farah Perelmuter** took an entrepreneurial leap of faith. They believed that the right speaker in front of the right audience could create lasting impact and that event planners, speakers, and audiences could be served in new and better ways. Since then, Speakers Spotlight has grown into one of the world's largest and most respected speakers agencies. With an incredible roster of speakers (including Scott), to date Speakers Spotlight has arranged more than 38,000 speaking engagements in over 50 countries and are thankful to have received many awards and accolades along the way.*

(Highlights from our interview, recorded June 14, 2023.)

MY NAME IS FARAH PERELMUTER, and I'm the CEO and cofounder of Speaker Spotlight. For over 20 years, I led the marketing team, and now, in addition to that, I work with my partner Martin and department heads on the overall development of the company. I also work with our lawyers, accountants, and banks on the high-level works of the business.

When I was six, my grandmother got me a T-shirt that said, "I am the boss."

At the beginning, we didn't really know what we were doing. Neither of us had been in any sort of leadership position; we'd never thought about building a company or a team. As the team grew, one of our motivations was to create a business where people would be happy and want to go to work. We both had come from jobs we hated for different reasons. You spend a lot of time at work, and we believe work should be a place you like going to; it sounds simple, but it doesn't happen by accident. Every organization has a culture, either by design or by default. We became very conscious of culture and the values we wanted to build the company around, what values are important to us as individuals and as a company, attracting people who share those values, making sure we communicate them to the team, and keeping ourselves and them accountable to those values. We needed to model the behavior we wanted to see and be accountable. Anyone can have great values on a website or wall somewhere, but if they aren't communicated and modeled for others, then they won't come into existence.

Especially in times of uncertainty, leaders need to be nimble, flexible, and solution-focused. In the speaking industry, we faced some big challenges when COVID started. Our whole industry changed quickly, and we had to adjust, assess, and react very fast. We have very specific business goals for Speaker Spotlight. Our sales team has their business goals, so we're very formulaic in terms of those numbers. For our life we have a clear vision of what we want our life to look like, but we operate by gut. Thankfully, Martin and I see life through the same lens and are very much on the same page, which makes life much easier. Within the first few months of starting the business, way back in 1995, we ripped up our business plan because it no longer made sense. It was immediately obsolete, and we've never made one since. Leaders need to be nimble and flexible because things change constantly, and you have to change all the time.

Through those turbulent times, we were able to provide leadership that was calm and confident. People appreciate solid leadership.

Many of our speakers are world-renowned leaders in various fields; learning from them is a major reason for our success. We have read their books, watched them speak, and got to know them personally. They're true professionals, who work to develop their business and are accommodating to clients. Leadership is about finding connections and then, over time, deepening those connections. You have to be able to listen and understand other people's concerns, learn their passions, and understand their needs.

I'm **Martin Perelmuter**, president and co-founder of Speaker Spotlight. We started 28 years ago, and my role has changed over the years. At the beginning it was mostly direct client work, and now I manage our sales team, making sure they have whatever support and direction they need. I also recruit new speaker talent, support existing talent, and handle overall management and leadership of the company.

Leadership starts with the human values we built the company around. This is especially important because of the type of business we're in. We aren't selling widgets, or a product—we're selling people sharing their stories and expertise, and it is all deeply personal. For us, an authentic alignment of those values, from the leadership through the organization, was critical. Although communication is important, it's what you do in leadership, not what you say. You can't just have meetings where you talk about values. Everybody from the newest, entry-level employee to the senior team has to see you acting those values; otherwise, they're lost; your team will become jaded and cynical. In addition to our actions, communication is best done through stories. For each of our values, we have stories that illustrate why they are important and how they play out in the real world. Doing the right thing and being true to your values may not always have an immediate result, but over the long run it works to your benefit. It's not only the right thing to do; it's a smart thing to do.

It sounds a bit cliché, but leaders aren't born; they're made. I've never considered myself a leader, and leading an organization or company was never something I wanted to do growing up. I played a lot of sports when I was younger, and I was always very happy to be one member of the team—give me my role, tell me what I need to do, and I'll do it! I never wanted to be the coach or the leader of a team. We didn't start the company to be leaders; it was a lifestyle decision for us and something we thought we could do well together. So I had insecurities as a leader, especially at the beginning, because I didn't see myself as one of those charismatic, inspirational leaders that can rally the troops and everything. Over time, I realized that is only one type of leadership, and many leaders I looked up to were actually introverted and humble. I realized I just had to be myself.

There are many different ways to lead effectively, and you have to be true to yourself. Making plans and taking courses in business and entrepreneurship is good to learn basic stills and frameworks, but when you get into the real world you need to be adaptable. We're more compass- than road-map-type people. We don't tell people how to get from point A to point B—instead we believe in shaping a general direction and figuring things out as we go. We can't always say exactly which route we're taking, but we know our stuff, are prepared, and trust ourselves and our team to figure things out together.

30

A Note: A Workplace Is Not a Family

AFTER HEARING FROM MEGAN, LUCKEY, Martin, and Farah, and considering who is writing this book, it is important to note that while family can be a part of business, a business is not a family. We spend a lot of time at work, but it is disingenuous and potentially dangerous for a leader to characterize work as a family. The label is often used in job postings or to welcome new arrivals (Welcome to the UnMarketing family!). To some, a family might denote respect, open communication, and shared vision—but that is taking a whole lot of things for granted. A family means different things to different people.

A family atmosphere can create an environment where roles are blurred and accountability is difficult to achieve because of an overexaggerated sense of loyalty. Employees can be taken advantage of and work beyond their capacities, leading to burnout. Furthermore, in a family environment, it is hard for constructive feedback not to feel personal. "You don't fire a family member, nor do you put them through performance improvement plans. Relationships between employees and employers are temporary in nature and at some point, have to come to an end. So to liken the relationship

to a family creates an allusion that the bond will last indefinitely"
(Luna 2021).

When workplace scandals are in the news, we often learn that
"everyone knew" what was going on, and ask why more people
didn't come forward to report. Their silence can be seen as selfish and unethical (which it may be); however, research shows that
"concern over the welfare of a person who commits a crime can pre-
vent whistleblowing, especially in close-knit groups" (Khan 2021).
Loyalty is something that is earned with trust over time. Rather
than focusing on a family, create structures and systems that foster open communication, feedback, accountability, and support.
Create a culture that supports fairness over loyalty, and loyalty will
come; bring your team around shared values, vision, and impact.

31

UnLeadership Is Driven by Values

EVERY LEADER WE SPOKE TO brought leadership back to values and meaning. Values are what get us up in the morning and keep going when things are hard. Values become stories we create or co-create with others—and these stories spread and tell others who we are, what we do, and why they should trust our vision. UnLeaders act their values by embracing innovations that make sense, keeping their values clear and using them to dictate practice. They make tough choices, take things like environmental responsibility seriously, and lead by example—from hiring to workplace design to setting out expectations and responsibilities. When your values align clearly with your company's activities, you are able to provide the kind of transparency that will set you apart. Success in the age of disruption isn't driven by the bottom line—it's value driven. Rather than looking quarter to quarter, ask yourself: "How would my business actions change if I thought about building a company to last 100 years?"

Like many of you, UnMarketing faced challenges (existential dread) over the last few years. In many ways, it brought us back to the days, and long nights, of starting the company. Limited resources, uncertainty, that moment at 2 a.m. when you look at yourself in the mirror and say, "My mom was right. I should have been a lawyer." We had to remember why we started and keep going; we had to decide what was most important and focus energy and resources there. We had to say no to anything that was not most important and be OK with losing those things. What is the opposite of a midlife crisis? We don't really have a word for it, do we? A glow-up perhaps, as the kids say. This is where you find us, all glowed up. A little bruised perhaps, but snark has always been our brand anyway. What emerged was a renewed focus on value. We asked ourselves:

What do we value, and how can we put those values into action every day?

What makes us feel valued in our work and our relationships?

How do we bring value to our customers, our communities, and the spaces we spend time in and off?

32

Leadership Momentum

FAE JOHNSTONE IS A TRAILBLAZING trans woman, queer advocate, and small business owner. She is a sought-after speaker, trainer, and writer on 2SLGBTQIA+ inclusion in Canada. She is a co-owner and executive director of Wisdom2Action—a national consulting firm specializing in community engagement, organizational development, and 2SLGBTQIA+ inclusion, and president of the Society of Queer Momentum—a national 2SLGBTQIA+ advocacy organization. Wisdom to Action was founded in 2011 and spent its first seven years as a federally funded knowledge mobilization network, working with children and bringing knowledge from academia into the youth-serving sector. In 2018, the executive director reimagined the organization as a consulting firm with a social enterprise commitment, and Fae was one of the first to join the team at that stage. They worked together until she was elected as a Member of the Legislative Assembly in Nova Scotia, and Fae became the sole executive director. About a year ago, they brought in a co-owner, Dennis Stubing, as Fae's second-in-command, so to speak.

When Wisdom to Action started, they were a small team doing good work with little business infrastructure. As they grew, they put core capacities in place regarding contracts for their growing team and scaled the work they were doing in a big way. Speaking with Alison about leadership, Fae shared that "the values and deficits of nonprofit work are that the cause is centered above everything else; there's an instinct to undersell yourself to get the work done and move the cause forward. We needed to ensure our employees are well compensated, thriving, and growing within their roles. We're still a small business, but the flexibility of our funding sources allows us to resource work in a way that others can't. We work with a model where leadership brings in the business, and we staff it with our project officers who retain a fair chunk of the nonprofit model and approach." This is an area in which Fae wants to develop the skills of their team further, to straddle that line more.

In her work, Fae values relationships and the products they produce beyond their baseline or capacity to make profits in a given contract. When they work with one client, they might leverage what they develop with them for a broader social purpose. "For example, we have developed tools over the years about 2SLGBTQ+ inclusion and trans suicide prevention. We mobilize those beyond our contractual relationship with the client, take pieces of work we value, and find funding sources to scale those alongside our clients. Our work is about justice, not just the detail of what we're hired to do." As a firm, Wisdom to Action incubated the idea of taking some of their expertise and putting it into a new home that would focus on queer and trans advocacy. They understood their skills would add value to the work—that they could bring a new lens and help meet the moment. They started the Society of Queer Momentum to scale their advocacy and nonprofit work more significantly.

One of Wisdom to Action's clients is Canadian Blood Services, which has a legacy of harm, homophobia, and transphobia. Because of that history, they've ruined a lot of relationships with queer and trans civil society and advocates. Only over the last year or so have they begun to change their position. Fae and her team have been working with them through a community engagement model, bringing stakeholders from queer and trans organizations into the conversation. "Rather than a quick focus group or one-off training, we offer sustained and ongoing support. We build trust and set clear parameters so that community members can speak out and criticize. We've helped them slowly build trust with the organizations they need to collaborate with to repair the harm they've caused. It is interesting to be the queer and trans consulting firm advocating and working with organizations that have caused harm. My favorite joke is that if you hate me for working with Canadian Blood Services, you can meet me outside the workshop with your pitchforks. But you'll have to fight the far-right people with their pitchforks first. Fun, right?"

Fae is also a board member for YWCA Canada and Oxfam Canada, two organizations near and dear to her heart. "As we see a rising tide of hate, many of the efforts from hate-motivated groups are to divide communities and pit us against one another. Working with the YWCA was an opportunity to support feminist liberation and a future that all our communities deserve. As a consultant, I've learned so much from the work of our more established feminist sibling organizations about how to navigate and respond to issues while remaining grounded in their values." Most people Fae works with are in their 20s and have courageous ideas about how the world should work versus the actual workplace landscape, where resources and capacity can be limited. Fae tries to help them navigate an aspirational lens with a pragmatic one: "We cannot change the world in a day, but we can create a context where change can happen. I've learned this from watching leaders I admire, like Paulette Senior, CEO of the Canadian Women's Foundation, and Debbie Owusu-Akyeeah, the executive director of the Canadian Center for Gender and Sexual Diversity."

Speaking with Fae about her leadership, she shared, "To do my work, I have to stay grounded and connected to the experiences of somebody on the East Coast, West Coast, and the prairies who's hanging out as the one out gay person in their town. I take as many opportunities as possible to be in different community contexts as possible because it's an opportunity to feel the pulse of the community and know people's worries, anxieties, and hopes. Those connections make me a better advocate and learn about local innovation that might otherwise not be on my radar. At the end of the day, the folks leading the fight for queer and trans justice are the folks in Fernie, BC, where they have an out United Church pastor where queer folks are creating the first and only pride space in their region. It is humbling in the best way to recognize that you are playing your part, but that role was made possible by elders who came before and the folks on the ground. I deal with a lot of doom and gloom, but I also see the joy in a 16-year-old trans kid's eyes and realize it might not have been possible when I was growing up. Staying grounded in that joy makes the work easier. For people coming up, first and foremost, trust your expertise and experience. If you're navigating the messy space of aspiration versus reality, stay grounded in your values while recognizing the goal you're working to achieve."

33

Be the Change Leadership

Amanda Hite is the cofounder and CEO of BTC (Be The Change) Revolutions, a social media marketing agency that specializes in engaging communities and igniting movements through their unique movement marketing model. For some of today's most innovative start-ups to well-known, multibillion-dollar businesses, BTC works with best-in-class brands who care about making a difference in the world, a people-driven marketing movement working on human media and intelligence. Amanda also launched Renaissance3, a company to run the platform Campaigns for Humanity. There, they identify global change-makers, take 25% of their profits, and put them into global funding campaigns.
(Highlights from our interview, recorded Aug 2, 2023.)

BEFORE STARTING MY OWN BUSINESSES, I worked in the corporate world of talent and human resources. My cofounder Brandon came from a similar background, and we both realized HR and marketing should be working together because both departments were people driven, and marketing had better budgets. When we landed our first huge brand client, we beat out all these big marketing agencies even though we were small and makeshift. We succeeded without traditional marketing experience because our human and talent resource training stood apart. People were the medium in this new social media space, and that has stayed the same even as social and digital media have changed.

We were obsessed with what we saw in the movement space on social media. As things were happening, like the Occupy movement or with President Obama's campaign, Brandon was tracking the data so we could study how it all worked. We took that data and began organizing people around those principles. One of the causes that was important to me because of my experience growing up was No Kid Hungry. Before they were clients, I volunteered for them, and they needed a social plan. We put together a social council, people from different backgrounds who were passionate about the cause, to see what we could learn. We created a people-driven social strategy with digital advocates who could share the cause and be involved in activations. We raised millions of dollars through social media and through the networks of advocates and communities who grew year after year. Around the same time, my friends and network from corporate were getting into higher positions and a pal, Kat Cole, gave us a shot with Cinnabon. We were figuring out how to put what we learned in the movement space and apply it to working with a brand.

I came out of conservative, corporate America and swung the other way: no dress code, results-focused workplace, unlimited time off, etc. We started out trying to make BTC the coolest, most meaningful and fun place to do good, but there needed to be balance. We focused on being "like a family," which became like a cult. Evolving through that meant realizing we were hiring people for a workplace, not a family. People wanted me to create a job that gave them more time, energy, and headspace to be with their loved ones. I had to learn that clarity was kind, to have tough conversations when needed, and infrastructure. As a leader, my job is to give meaningful work, help others grow, and create an environment where you are thriving and flourishing, which can also be shut off when you leave. When leading a company, you should always be cocreating and evolving with the feedback of the people around you.

Without question, COVID-19 rocked the whole world. With many of our clients in the restaurant industry, there were a lot of shutdowns and disruptions. We had a responsibility to demonstrate being people-first, and we decided to push for no layoffs and communicate this along the way to employees. We were flexible. When clients wanted out of contracts, we let them know they could pay what they could, give it a few months, and see. We looked at the worst-case scenario—closing the company down—and decided if we were going to go out, we'd go out with a bang and help our employees along the way. Later, when the government sent out checks, we matched those for our employees and could give raises. It was hard, but we had to act decisively and according to our values. We asked ourselves, "What does the world need right now, and how can we help with that?" and began working around COVID and vaccine disinformation. When we named the company, people gave us hell because we weren't a charity or nonprofit; we were doing marketing. But Brandon and I created the company we always wanted to work for: to make a vehicle for change and help improve people's lives. We wanted to maintain that focus and wanted the name to remind us of that every day. When it's been hard, when we've been more focused on our bottom line, we ask ourselves, "Are we being the change right now?"

I grew up a queer kid in a conservative Southern Baptist home, living in 32 houses by age 18; there was a lot of hardship and adversity. When I got into the workforce, my number one goal was independence. Then, one day, I looked around an executive table and realized no one was happy. There had to be something more meaningful out there. When I was younger, I thought the title was the thing that would give me credibility and respect, but that's not a guarantee. I have learned people respect you because of how you treat them, how you invest in them, and how much they believe you care. Leadership isn't a title. As we organize for causes, we look around the room for the person making the biggest impact and often assume they're the loudest person with the biggest title. But when you look closer, you see quiet people doing the work of organizing. Leadership needs to be redefined. If you want examples, look beyond your workplace. I think about my grandfather or one of my best friends, Sharon, who is the biggest badass. We can't live enough lives to have all the experience we need to lead us out of the world's most complex problems, so read and learn. The world is desperate for leaders, especially those who come from the heart and care about doing the right thing. If you are reading this and think you're not ready to be a leader but are inspired to lead, start now. Just step into it.

34

Leadership Practice

Alex Battick is an education lawyer who practices in Ontario, giving legal advice and support to stakeholders in the education system. His clients include students, families, employers, and organizations from kindergarten to higher education. His firm, Battick Legal Advisory, has built its reputation as leaders in Ontario's educational law landscape, providing expert advice and representation in administrative, employment, human rights, and regulatory issues.
(Highlights from our interview, recorded July 10, 2023.)

IN ENGLAND, WHERE I STUDIED law, there was a unique opportunity for law students to advocate for and support students who had been excluded (synonymous with expulsion here). The program allowed us hands-on experience advocating for students and their families without "training wheels," or established lawyers doing the work. I come from a family of educators, so perhaps there was always this silent push; I knew I didn't want to be a teacher, but working within education was something I enjoyed and wanted to focus on more. I returned to Canada and went to work at a legal aid clinic, and although education law was a part of the practice, I found no type of service with that specific and exclusive focus. Any area of law with a descriptor, like sports law, health law, etc., is industry-specific.

The law you're practicing might be contract, constitutional, or administrative—all these different areas of law brought under the context of a specific industry. When I started my firm five years ago, there wasn't a model or framework to copy. I started with a shallow idea based on my experience and built from there, based on feedback from clients who would come to me asking for things they needed support with. I had to evolve with my clients' needs. For example, as clients came in needing human rights support or employment issues, I learned how to apply each area within the education industry.

The work I do depends on the client. I have individual clients for whom the opposing party is typically the school, organization, or institution of learning. In those circumstances, the organization has seemingly infinite resources. My role is to help clients navigate the system, guiding them through the most effective and efficient process, internally or externally, to hopefully get the outcome they are looking for. I also have clients who are organizations. For example, a private school is concerned about its position in mitigating human rights liability. I would work with them to figure out policies and practices and to create a framework within which they can work to best follow the human rights code. Historically, there has been an unwillingness to provide resources for families to advocate for themselves within the school system and student discipline, and very few decisions are appealed. This was an area where I could take my specialized knowledge.

A few years ago, one of my students, who had also studied in England, came to me looking for volunteer opportunities and hands-on experience. We created CARE Student Advocacy, a pro bono legal support initiative operated by law students that provides support for parents of students who need assistance with formal communications with schools. Wanting to have more impact, as an articling student, I joined the board of Rexdale Community Health

Center. Boards need subject matter experts, and I tell young lawyers to get involved in board work. It is helpful for organizations to have a legal perspective and, selfishly, a great experience for a young lawyer to learn, network, and show a record of their commitment to the community. I am also part of the 1834 Fellowship, an organization that supports Black students interested in federal policy work. I'll have a new student every few months, and we explore professional and personal issues; I really enjoy the mentee-mentor relationship. Books are also great mentors; Tim Ferriss and Robert Green's writing on apprenticeship and mastering your craft come to mind. Books have given me different perspectives and made a big impact on where I am today. Although, it's funny because some books say if you wanna run your own law firm, you have to decide between being a lawyer or a business person. Advice isn't meant to be a template; if something vibes with you, take what you need and don't copy-paste.

When it comes to growing my practice, I think about Paul Jarvis's book *The Company of One*. He talks about the danger of growth, constantly shifting your goals for more. I'm not drawn to becoming a big firm and the lifestyle it would take to get there. My path is to become a subject matter expert and the go-to resource for this small area of specialization I've chosen. My idea of growth is becoming a resource for challenging questions at the intersection of education and law. The North Star for my practice has been, "All you need to do is survive until the next big opportunity." There are highs and lows, especially with a niche practice. In the first few years, I was figuring things out, and the idea of getting to the next opportunity kept me going. Survival as a business owner requires lots of pivoting, adjusting, learning, adapting, and figuring out what you could do better. From the jump, know that you'll face barriers and challenges. The key is knowing the next opportunity will come. Courage is a huge aspect of leadership. When I started, I didn't see law practices like the one I wanted to build, but I knew there was a need. The world is big; you only need a small percentage of people to be interested in your idea. You don't need everyone on your side or everyone to agree with you; build it, and they will come.

35

Leading in Beauty

Jenn Harper *is the founder and CEO of Cheekbone Beauty Cosmetics, an Indigenous-owned beauty brand paving the way in truly sustainable product development and manufacturing in the cosmetics space. The brand is known for its sustainable and high-quality color cosmetics that are clean, vegan, and cruelty free. Jenn is a sought-after speaker for corporations, businesses, and students across North America. She champions entrepreneurship, building a sustainable brand using Indigenous roots, the history of her Indigenous family, and lots more.*
(Highlights from our interview, recorded June 12, 2023.)

WHEN BUILDING YOUR OWN THING, you get to choose what kind of company you want to build and how it will look and feel. Compassion and humility aren't qualities we always consider with leadership, but they should be. I'm an Anishinaabe woman, meaning I come from the Ojibwe tribe, and my people have surrounded the Great Lakes for thousands of years. I get to live and work on the territory known as the Niagara region in southern Ontario, Canada, the traditional homelands of the Haudenosaunee and the Anishinaabe people. In the early days of my business, it was just me and a dream. It takes time to evolve into the entrepreneur you want to be, so I did a lot of learning and research. I was drawn to social entrepreneurship, which was still new when we started in 2015. At the same time, I was also learning more about my culture and Indigenous teachings and was excited to find alignment. We use the Seven Grandfather teachings as the foundation for our business. These values guide our decisions and go beyond leadership to reach everyone so our workspace feels safe, friendly, healthy, and happy. We want our customers to have a certain feeling when using our products, when making purchases, and when visiting spaces we're in. That requires a strong vision and communicating it to our team so it is shared.

We're built on three pillars. Our Indigenous roots define our vision and are fundamental to everything we do. Second is environmental sustainability, which is part of being Indigenous. Third, we bring bold, clean colors to a category that has been a muted space for too long. These pillars shape everything, from our customer service to our packaging, which is vibrant and sustainable. Indigenous people have been the keepers of land for thousands of years, generation after generation. We see this today worldwide, where Indigenous peoples protect the rainforest and protest pipelines. We recognize environmental sustainability is a massive issue. I never want to pretend that, as one brand, we have all the answers or can solve this problem alone. But it is our job to make people aware there are options, different ways, and choices. We are honest about our products' impact and believe in being transparent about impact. There's a lot of nuanced information, and it can be more complex than not using plastics or a certain material; there is a huge learning curve and a lot of innovation in the space.

I've seen positive changes in the beauty industry, even Cheekbone's success so far, in an industry run by about five companies, led mostly by white men who live in France somewhere. There are more women and women of color taking leadership positions within organizations. I see better messaging, a world where our children can grow up feeling beautiful no matter their shape, size, and skin tone. Our brand has always been about feeling—we want people to feel good about using our products and themselves. The beauty industry has a vital role in how we feel about ourselves, and seeing larger companies now recognize that and make campaigns around that messaging is super important. We're on the right path. Even in the early days of Cheekbone, I recognized the power of social media and how it could be used for good to connect and show customers how we operated. Although it has evolved over the years, we have a lot of fun with it and see more and more people finding us through TikTok. Talking to our Sephora teams across the country, they confirmed people now come in with their phones open, looking for their favorite brands. This has been a shift in consumer behavior that dictates our mission—to curate better products for people and the planet. Yes, we are a serious company with goals and vision, but we also want to share joy. We want to create opportunities for customers to see behind the scenes what it's like to operate a small business. We are open and honest.

I never did well in secular school or education; it was always a struggle. The more time I spent with other Indigenous entrepreneurs and academics, the more I learned that sometimes systems were not designed for us. Learning is a powerful part of our journey as human beings, and being educated can help you define the life you want to create for yourself, your family, and your community. I saw that within our communities, the education system was failing a lot of Indigenous learners. It can be frustrating when problems seem bigger than one person or company can solve. But we were growing as a brand, and I wanted to be part of making positive change. We created our scholarship fund to give Indigenous youth more educational choices based on who they were and their needs at the time. Even though it can be challenging, representing Cheekbone has transformed me in many ways, giving me a new goal and purpose: to be a role model to aspiring Indigenous entrepreneurs.

I have been sober since 2014, which shapes a big part of my daily practice. I always start my day being physically active or in nature. If the weather is bad, or I don't have much time, I will stand in a patch of grass for a few seconds or do breathing exercises to feel that connection. After nine years of sobriety, that routine has been built in; it's part of my system, keeping me in the flow and on track for the rest of the day. My team is still small, but we have a weekly meeting to discuss work, share new ideas, and envision them together. When work is challenging, I think of a young person who isn't sure what they want to do with their lives. Maybe they're struggling, and they see me and think, "She struggled too, but she made it. She did something with her life and was able to do it in a way that we call, as Ojibwe people say, having a life and doing right."

36

Leadership Hospitality

Alejandro Castro-Alfaro *specializes in marketing, strategy, business consulting and sustainable development focused in the tourism industry. His passion for the environment and responsible business drove him to co-lead the "I Dare You To Plant A Tree" campaign, one of the largest private-public initiatives ever carried out in the country for this matter. He founded the INCAE MBA Oath Club—the first graduate level business ethics club in Latin America. Upon completing his MBA, Alejandro assumed a leadership role within his family business (public transportation and tourism). In 2014 the minister of tourism of Costa Rica appointed him as the youngest deputy manager and marketing director of the Tourism Board (ICT). After this governmental role, Alejandro transitioned into independent consultant and established his own business consulting firm and an advertising agency. Alejandro has worked as an international business consultant with Grameen Creative Lab (Colombia) and with THR Tourism Industry Advisors (Spain/ Saudi Arabia) and actively invested in local entrepreneurs.*

(Highlights from our interview, recorded June 7, 2023.)

IT'S INTERESTING TO THINK ABOUT leadership. There is a big difference between leading within a company, the public sector, or a political organization and trying to get your mother to restructure the family business. My grandfather was a pioneer, and I've been trying to change the company since my early 20s—so I have certainly learned a lot along the way, especially about the challenges of leading at a young age. I had to be entrepreneurial and build myself up to prove my leadership. Although I always wanted to be data driven, I needed to learn that emotional things keep companies together, growing and making good decisions. Everything isn't business—I went in trying to reach my own tactical and innovative objectives, but I had to learn how to get people on my side.

One of my first leadership experiences was in 2007 when I was part of leading the campaign "A que sembrás un árbol, I dare you to plant a tree." The prince of Monaco and Wangari Maathai, who had been awarded the Nobel Peace Prize for founding the Green Belt Movement in Kenya, had started the Billion Tree Campaign, and a friend brought me in to start a Costa Rican chapter. Our plan was interdisciplinary, with 10 or so institutions collaborating to plant and geo-reference. In the first year, we planted and pinned around 5.9 million trees; in the second year, 7 million; and in the third, about 7.3 million. I was in university, going to school during the day and working on marketing at night. The government had money for tree planting but wasn't aligned with suppliers and planters. We connected people wanting to plant with the institution through marketing, and boom, we had an amazing campaign. The planted trees mainly were native species, and the campaign supported sustainable wood production, protection, the recovery of hydrographic basins, biodiversity, urban beautification, and awareness. For a young person, it was an incredible learning experience. Being authentic is the greatest power a leader can have. When I later became the youngest deputy manager of the Ministry of Tourism, I struggled to earn respect by fitting in. But that wasn't me; I had to learn to be myself and trust that I could implement my ideas and follow my values.

By 2020, I had gained international experience and confidence; the company had a perfect plan, and all these skill sets were coming together—and then COVID hit, and everything shut down. Not a single plane was landing in Costa Rica. The company shifted. We invested in an abandoned hotel in Guanacaste, and I went to work, making it more touristic. We separated from my uncle, who kept the public transportation part of the company, and we kept the tourist assets that needed developing. We innovated using a methodology, "Think Wrong to Solve Next." We did drills and meetings with the whole family to ensure we were aligned. In the end, we made a list of who we wanted to be as a company; we called it DonDa, after my grandfather Danilo Alfaro Campos. Don means "mister," and Da is a diminutive of Danilo. Da also means "give," and my grandfather gave loans without collateral to help people in our community. At his funeral, so many people approached me to thank my grandfather for getting them a house and making sure they had jobs or went to school. That's the reason I love DonDa—because it also means Mr. Give. Since then, our decisions have been aligned with the values on that list. As you grow as a leader and have more power and influence, you need to stay true to your principles and have non-negotiables. My values are my North Star, keeping me on track.

One important value for me was creating experiences, to be aligned with the community, grow with it, and make it a better place. We work with the community to choose tour operators, find the most pristine areas, and ensure the community we work with has a better life. There have been challenges; I went from being an international player in tourism to the little town of Santa Cruz, trying to build up a small business. People couldn't understand why I was there, but I believed in the DonDa personification. My passion for Costa Rica, all the beautiful places and people here is a huge component of my leadership. Right now, in tourism, everyone is talking about storytelling and experience generation, which comes naturally when you share something you love and are connected to. Costa Rica may be little, but we can show how things can be done differently. We have the Pura Vida vibe, and we need to spread it more in the world.

The digital world is becoming less human, but tourism is about human connections. People travel to see beautiful places, experience a culture, have a personal touch, and understand life in another part of the world. We have to be special and develop a unique experience. Costa Rica is beautiful, but we have to go beyond that. We need to treat tourists as we'd want to be treated and put ourselves in their shoes. When designing an experience, I'm always thinking about feeling, and your staff needs to be on board to pass it along to the customer. Every day, I try to be the best version of myself and transmit my passion to others. With any decision, I ask myself, "Will I be proud?"

When something I say or accomplish is in the local newspaper, I ask myself, "What will my family think of it?" You can't always be right, and you'll make mistakes, but your values and non-negotiables shape your decisions.

37

UnLeadership Pathways

THERE ARE MANY PATHWAYS TO leadership. We spoke with leaders who'd gone through traditional schooling and others who did not. Some climbed the corporate ladder, and quit and never looked back. We spoke to authors, speakers, and creators who are driven to share their messages, no matter the medium. No matter the pathway, whether working in for-profit, nonprofit, or social enterprise spaces, UnLeaders are guided by values and impact.

Even within the traditional workplace, we've seen a shift. Although there have been economic changes since the beginning of the Great Resignation, the percentage of workers who report they are planning to leave their jobs has stayed the same, around 40% since 2021. What we are seeing is a mismatch between the demand for talent and the number of workers willing to supply it. "Employers continue to rely on traditional levers to attract and retain people, including compensation, titles, and advancement opportunities. Those factors are important, particularly for a large reservoir of workers we call 'traditionalists.' However, the COVID-19 pandemic has led more and more people to reevaluate what they want from a job—and from life—which is creating a large pool of active and potential workers who are shunning the traditionalist path" (McKinsey & Company 2022).

We're reshuffling, reinventing, and reassessing. People want flexibility and freedom regardless of the job, workplace, or industry. Rather than a cool kitchen or games room, flexibility is the amenity workers want. That means employers must look at workflow and processes and rethink how they get things done. In a traditional workplace, people are often promoted into managerial and leadership positions because they are skillful and good team members. Without additional leadership skills (awareness, connection, empathy, etc.) and support and training, great doers can easily become problematic managers. Leadership is given as a reward—however, as we have seen, leadership is a responsibility first. Some companies, such as online HR platform Remote, are offering two pathways for promotion: one where someone becomes a manager, and another where they remain an individual contributor, but with an equal growth in compensation. We love policies like this because they recognize the unique tool kit required for leadership, that not everyone wants or is suited for the role, and also provide advancement outside the traditional company structure.

According to a 2021 Workplace Happiness Study commissioned by Indeed and conducted by Forrester Consulting, nearly half of people believe the expectations of happiness at work have increased over the last five years, and 97% of people believe happiness at work is possible (Work Happiness Survey 2021). Rather than a Great Resignation, Indeed calls this the "Great Realization." Today, people want the opportunity for healthier, happier work environments and lives. The focus on well-being is even more critical during transition and change. The study worked with leading wellness experts to create a list of key drivers of happiness. These included a sense of belonging, feeling energized by work tasks, being appreciated, feeling as if work has a clear purpose, opportunities for learning and advancement, flexibility, and trust. After pay, which was the number one driver for leaving a job and which should be thought of as a fundamental need (instead of a driver of happiness), these were the reasons people stayed, maintained their well-being, and thrived at work.

As Annie Dillard wrote in *The Writing Life*, "How we spend our days is, of course, how we spend our lives." And we spend a tremendous amount of our time at work. For aspiring leaders, change means the sky's the limit. There is no right or wrong way to lead or take your values and find a path toward the impact you want.

38

A Note: Work-Life Balance

WHEN WE BEGAN WORKING ON UnLeadership, we knew we wanted to disrupt the idea of work-life balance and that emotions have no place in business. Business is personal. We all want work that brings us fulfillment and challenge, and at the end of the day, we can leave behind knowing we can care for and support those we care about. We move forward more successfully by encouraging and facilitating leadership at every level.

Setting boundaries around work hours can be very challenging in our modern world. This can be both a good thing and a challenge. For leaders (particularly entrepreneurs), being constantly connected can allow work hours and location flexibility. As an employee, being always at the beck and call of email and clients can come at a cost.

It's wonderful that we can work from anywhere at any time.

It's terrible that we can work from anywhere at any time.

One key to work-life balance is setting sustainable expectations we can manage. This means open communication channels within a company, where workers can express concerns about overtime demands and management can lay out clear expectations. These expectations need to be shared with customers so that they know about wait times for responses and product and service delivery. When we know when we can expect a reply, we're much less likely to get angry about a late one. As a leader, you must respect your team, clients, and customers enough to share your best work. If your product or service doesn't demand a 24/7 mentality (like an emergency plumbing company, for example), emails do not require a response on Sunday at 11:05 p.m. We're pretty sure your marketing clients can wait until Monday. Maybe it's time to hire more people? If you've decided 24/7 is your thing, you can only stretch your employees so far before they break. This isn't the time or place to save—hire more employees to lessen the load and improve your overall service. You may think you're growing profits, but you're actually lowering the value of your business.

As a leader, cut yourself some slack. When your work is driven by value and impact, work-life balance is often no more than a facade. Spend time deciding what's important to you, make time for that, and focus. Leaders need to balance the time they need away from work with the flexibility and constant contact modern technology has allowed us. These needs vary tremendously between people—there is no one way to succeed at a life-work balance. We spend a tremendous amount of our lives at work. Decide what it means to you, and move toward that. For us, work-life balance is about filling our time with meaningful, creative work that allows us to spend time with our family, supporting others and things we care about, and laughing a lot, no matter what we're doing.

39

Leadership and Influence

Las Vegas is one of our favorite places, and if you know us, then you know we always like to include a little Vegas in our books. Way back in the early 2010s, Scott sent out a tweet asking his followers to guess the name of the '80s hair metal band he was listening to. Whoever guessed right, Scott promised to buy them lunch next time he was in their city for a speaking gig. Typical answers came in (you're probably saying them right now): Poison, Mötley Crüe, etc. Then a reply came in that simply said, "Stryper?" And Scott had a winner, **Mike Snedegar**, who along with his musical clairvoyance, also happened to live in Las Vegas and, as you'll see, knows a few things about the entertainment industry.

Mike is the entertainment marketing director for TAO Group Hospitality, based in Las Vegas. Alison sat down with Mike to talk about leadership, here are some highlights from our interview recorded.

(Highlights from our interview, recorded July 10, 2023.)

MY NAME IS MIKE SNEDEGAR and my job is to create, maintain, and expand upon relationships with people in the entertainment industry that carry a certain amount of influence. That could be an actor, musician, rapper, pop star, influencer, athlete, someone in the adult film industry, an agent, manager, or publicist, anybody that carries influence in the world of entertainment. I create a relationship between the influential person and Tao Group and introduce them to our brands if unfamiliar. We want them to feel comfortable and eventually become organic brand marketers. I want to weave them into the fabric of the brand, and hopefully they can bring others to experience it.

I started working for Tao Group in 2005 as an assistant to one of the owners, Jason Strauss, who is now co-CEO. I was a VIP host in Vegas then, working at two nightclubs and writing a column for a nightlife magazine. The magazine asked me to write an editorial about Jason, and we met and went out a few times that week to hang out. Back then, Tao wasn't the massive hospitality company it is today. I knew the brand was a celebrity hotspot from a *Sex and the City* episode, where Carrie and all go to Tao in New York City. I did my research, spent time learning Jason's day-to-day, and came to understand his and his partner Noah Tepperberg's work and loved everything they were trying to do in Las Vegas. Because I knew so many local clientele, Jason initially offered me a job as a host, but I said no, that I would rather be his assistant. I cut my income in half, which ended up being the best thing I ever did. Becoming Jason's assistant, and taking those three steps back, moved me miles ahead. I helped Jason balance his schedule and sometimes had to run a PR call, format ads, or run events. It was a sink-or-swim environment, which I learned to thrive on. My background as a VIP host meant that I had worked with celebrities before, so Jason often had me work with their requests.

Las Vegas nightlife was growing rapidly. Programming became important, and incorporating celebrities helped drive traffic. People from *The Hills*, MTV, or different shows would come in, create an ad, and host the nightclub. I had an idea to do an event with a girl I'd met once or twice, named Kim Kardashian. There was no

TV show yet; she was known as Paris Hilton's friend at that time. It took some convincing because not everyone was on board, but it went well and got a lot of press. I loved creating the whole thing, all the moving parts of the wheel, from organizing to negotiations. The event was like a living, breathing thing; you had to have your hands in every aspect. I moved from my assistant job into the marketing department and began focusing on talent, celebrity, and bookings full-time.

For many years I booked talent, mainly rappers and hip-hop performers. I thought of who would be relevant for the moment, who would sell tickets and be a viable artist. I put together offers, negotiated contracts, and then, once that was done, oversaw the creation of artwork, logistics and hospitality, soundcheck, red carpet, and executing the performance. I worked with many of the biggest performers in the world. Right before the pandemic, I was about to get a promotion, when everything was put on hold. Gratefully, I didn't lose my job and was transferred to overseeing PR and social media. COVID gave me time to pause, and I realized I wanted a change. Now I work more hybridly in influencer marketing, PR, and pop-up activations like Coachella. I recently hosted the Wrexham soccer team, the one Ryan Reynolds is a part of. They won this game, Ryan flew them to Las Vegas to celebrate, and it got huge international press. Many of the team had never been to Las Vegas before, and when they saw Omnia nightclub, their faces were amazing. The experiential aspect of nightlife in Vegas is at a different level than anywhere else; it's mind-blowing.

There was a time when I went out constantly; two events in a day, a busy schedule, it was wild. I did that for a long time, but now things are different. I have those busy periods, but I'm not out 24/7 like I used to be. Part of that is learning from experience. There have been many events, difficult negotiations, and deals that went badly and caused me so much stress. At the time, it seemed like the end of the world, but now I look back and barely remember it. I went through a rocky period where my drinking was affecting my work. Jason and Noah took the time to come to me and say, "Are you OK? Can we help you?" I am so grateful for that. I've been sober for 10 years now, and Jason has become more than my boss; he is a huge figure in my life, not only as a mentor but a friend. I struggled a lot, being confident and not feeling like a leader because of things from my childhood and being bullied a lot. Everybody can be a leader; they just need that person to be there and tell them, "You can do it."

I'm from Lexington, Kentucky. I loved growing up there and still love it, but I knew I wanted something that wasn't there. You can live in a small town and get a job in entertainment, work at the local TV or radio station, but it depends on the level of business you want to be part of. I moved to Vegas in 2001, and the only person I knew here was my grandmother; I was so broke I couldn't even get my hair cut. I just started and made my way through. Trust your instincts; you want to work with people you can learn from and become better by being around. If you have a mentor or boss who isn't a good person, trust your gut on that too. Consistency equals longevity. There have been many times when I felt stuck professionally, and I've gotten through by staying the course. We often focus on what we want in the day-to-day, but it will only come to you when you're ready. And sometimes, it comes when you aren't ready for it, and that's when you learn the most.

40

A Leadership Franchise

*For 34 years, **Allan Hill** has been part of Domino's Pizza in Canada. Starting as a manager in training, he quickly embraced the business, attitudes, and community. Over the years he's been a manager, franchise operations director, national operations director, and finally franchisee, as the owner of stores in Lindsay, Toronto, Kingston, and Peterborough. Having now divested from all but his three Peterborough locations, Allan is enjoying more time to focus on family and community. His goal is for his customers not only to buy from Domino's Pizza but Allan Hill's Domino's Pizza. His family, team, and local community means everything to him.*

(Highlights from our interview, recorded June 2, 2023.)

MY NAME IS ALLAN HILL. Thirty-four years ago, I was hired as a manager in training at a Domino's location I now own. It was the only store in the area then, owned by Ian Toms, who became my mentor and friend. For 10 weeks, I ate and slept at Domino's and took every opportunity to learn from Ian, who taught me things I still use in my work and personal life today. A year later, I was offered a position as operational director. It was intimidating; everyone I met had more experience than me. I learned to lead with curiosity and focus on each store's best practices. When I later became a franchisee myself, the years of traveling store to store gave me a strong foundation to work from.

One of the things I love about being in a franchise is that Domino's has systems and suppliers in place; I don't have to reinvent the wheel. I've used those supports to free myself up to do what I want, to personalize, so it isn't just Domino's—it's Allan Hills Domino's Pizza in Peterborough. Having been a franchisee for 25 years in a small town, I'm very well known. I go just about everywhere with a logo on my shirt. I want people to know it's me when I go into a Walmart, to the hockey game, etc. I can't come up with Allan's favorite pizza and market that. But that's okay, I don't need to.

I've seen a lot of transformation in business. Technology has been life-altering for franchisees, managers, and everyone. When I started, we were handwriting everything, and I needed to know the cost of every pizza, every topping, off the top of my head. Now computers do all that. I remember bringing computers in for order taking the first time in Peterborough. The first month, everyone hated them because we all had so much to learn and change. By the second month, computers were OK; by the third, no one knew what to do without them. Whenever a new technology is introduced, Domino's offers support and operation coaches, or area leaders make personal visits. Now, we have AI technology that gives us notice before a customer finishes their order. Our studies showed that 95% of people who get to the payment page will finish the order so that information is sent to the store for us to get started. Before we had computers, based on our regulars, we thought the average customer ordered once every single week. However, ordering data showed us that 80% of our customers order five times a year. We use this data when we talk about increasing sales; if we can get them to order even once more a year, we've raised our sales by 20%.

I want to leave this planet knowing the world is better in a small way because I was here; that value drives my work. I give back to the community, volunteer with Junior Achievement, and take an interest in the people who work for me. Part of that is celebrating employee successes at work and in their personal lives. Their lives don't stop with work or with working for me; I want them to continue on and do great things. It's wrong when managers change their attitude toward workers after they give notice because their coworkers are watching, and you lose the opportunity to keep a great connection. One of the things I say to my managers is, "Once a Dominoid, always a Dominoid." I employ a lot of young people and international students working to get their permanent residency. They want to be Canadian citizens, and I want to do whatever I can to help make that happen and be part of helping them achieve their goals. I want them to look back at this time in their lives and remember working for Domino's Pizza in Peterborough as one of their best chapters.

When we interview potential managers, we talk about the fact that they will make mistakes and accept they may cost me more than their salary when they start out, and that's OK. Of course, I'm not looking for anyone to waste my money, but mistakes are not the end of the world. When we make mistakes, it affects customers, and we have to make that right. My goal every day is to give away a free pizza, and sometimes, my goal ends up being repeated because we're not perfect. When a customer has a problem, and they're in the store, the most senior person steps up to take care of them. I don't want managers hiding behind a kid, leaving them to deal with an angry customer. Being a manager is a servant position, not an authoritarian one.

Years ago, I had a team member named Steven. He was a high school student, and when he started, he was late to every shift. Rather than firing him or letting this continue, I sat down and explained the whole schedule. How we plan for busy times and how when he's late, someone else has to pick up the slack. It was his first job, and the first time anyone explained the reasons. From then on, he showed up on time, became assistant manager, and now works in an entirely different business, but we've remained friends. Everyone learns at a different pace; as a leader, you have to be patient and expect mistakes. I never give up unless the employee does.

41

Gold Record Leadership

Joel Carriere is the owner of Dine Alone Records, Bedlam Music Management, and New Damage Records. Launched in 2005, Dine Alone is a Canadian and American independent record label and event space, founded in St. Catharines and Toronto and now based in Toronto, Nashville, and Los Angeles. Joel has worked with artists such as Alexisonfire, City and Colour, Bedouin Soundclash, the Lumineers, and Arkells and new artists NOBRO, Cam Kahin, and EKKSTACY. Joel also happens to be our son Aidan's boss ("The best boss I've ever had").

(Highlights from our interview, recorded July 27, 2023.)

GROWING UP, I HAD A lot of interests, but music was always in the foreground. I was always the guy making mixed tapes at a young age and bringing cassettes to parties. I started going to concerts in my early teens, and they were the greatest thing I'd ever experienced. Everyone was together in the moment, enjoying it. There were no phones back then, so the experience was more about togetherness than individual moments.

Being from St. Catharines, I didn't have a lot of examples to guide me, or at least I didn't think I did at the time. I got a job at a record store and learned the ins and outs of the business, about buying patterns and taking risks in buying. The more passionate I was, the more I sold. I wasn't trying to be a salesperson; I just wanted people to check out the music I loved. A rep from Polygram gave me a shot right out of college as a customer service representative. I threw record release parties for artists like Shania Twain and Matthew Good. We'd grab 50 stores, check stock, put up installations, and work out pricing. It was a lot of fun, and I was learning the reverse side of retail marketing, data collection, and seeing what worked and what didn't. When Universal Records bought Polygram, I was laid off. I still had a bunch of jobs—DJing at a bar and helping throw concerts, stuff like that.

Although I'd learned a different side of the business at each step, I never felt like I was fully listened to. Back in college, I'd had a brainstorm for Bedlam Society, a counter-culture site that went against everything big-box and major label. I began collecting emails from shows in Buffalo and Niagara, hitting up labels and running contents. I shared my opinions on music, included some '80s movie quotes, and began getting a following. Promoters saw an interest and realized I had a group of people who followed me, listened to me, and came to shows. We created a website to go with the email list, and the whole thing caught on; we were promoting the smallest bands alongside Iron Maiden.

During all of this, around 2000, I began working with Alexisonfire. As Bedlam grew, we sold ads, mainly to Live Nation promoters, and became more involved in concerts. We took over the Scene Festival and partnered with Distort and House of Blues. We were doing shows in St. Catharines and pulling 400 all-age kids on a weekend; a place that had never been big became a spot for music that could make lots of money. I started scaling, doing shows in Toronto, and forming a social network. We realized we could take a whole punk rock tour and go across Canada, use our network to get the word out and not rely on big media, which might not cover it otherwise. We figured out how to launch music videos. This was before YouTube, and Much Music was popular but difficult to get on. Our audience could see music videos on our website, early Queens of the Stone Age stuff, which was wild then. In hindsight, we were really ahead of the curve.

Alexis was getting traction, and we were putting them through the Bedlam system, when I got a job for a big, UK-based label called Sanctuary Records. My friend Adam Sewell, the singer for Monster Voodoo Machine, recognized what I'd been doing and gave me the job. There, I was able to assist in marketing with Queensrÿche, Superjoint Ritual, which is made up of Pantera and Black Sabbath, and also a ton of horrible bands. Message board culture was big, and when I wasn't working, I was creating conversations about everything I was doing on the boards to get people talking. It was a lot of work, but something for me was fermenting. We serviced Alexis's first video, my partner Greg started the record label, and I became their manager. At the time, there was a show called PunchMuch, which let people vote for their favorite band. I traveled across the country, talking about this young, heavy band on PunchMuch, and people voted; Alexis went to number one in Canada.

My next band was Bedouin Soundclash, a reggae ska band with the biggest song in Canada at the time, who I helped navigate signing to the US record label SideOneDummy Records. Then Dallas Green from Alexis wanted to put out a solo album. This was the time to finally start my own label; that way, there would be two separate artists with two teams, and I was the nucleus for them both. We made Dallas's record and launched Dine Alone. Tricia Ricciuto and Lesley Benchina came on and helped me look at the company from a different perspective. Outside of having fun and being in music, I could make money and pay people well, which really cemented when we brought in Lisa Logutenkow. Together, we started moving the company forward.

We've been around 20 years, so there have been ups and downs. When I started, I would have a grand idea and run with it. But as you grow, you need to bring in others who understand situations better than you do. You grow for knowledge and need experts and specialists. We contract some gigs and hire people to lead production, art, marketing, etc. When you have a gold record and manage globally, you need people to come in and pay attention to marketing, managing bands, distribution, and running the label. Companies that aren't willing to grow, fail. Today the tools we use to collect data have changed, and we can be more analytical, but the passion and idea are still the same. We now have employees designated to buy online ads, do target marketing, and operate our social media, but it is the same ethos.

We pay attention to the market and adapt and never short-change ourselves. We've worked with bands who've sold millions of records; there's nothing we can't handle. Dine Alone started at the height of MySpace and Napster, and the whole music industry thought we were wrong, but to me, it was a perfect time because I had nothing to lose. Music is something people can get very wealthy from, but it's also just a great job to have. It's not always the highest-paying gig, but if you love music, there are other perks, like concerts, meeting bands, and being a part of growing something cool. Culturally, you get to see something ferment, be created, and have a touch point within it. I started out doing 10 different jobs, but they were all about music. Other leaders in the industry, the president of Live Nation or Universal, have the same story; we all did as much as we could and surrounded ourselves with people doing what we wanted to do. Find your lane, grow your knowledge, and make sure you can move beyond a growth spurt. Follow your passion, be logical, learn, and be able to adapt. Everything changes.

42

Leadership, a Founder's Story

Erin Bury is the CEO and cofounder of Willful and is the former managing director at Eighty-Eight, a Toronto-based creative communications agency. Before Eighty-Eight she was the managing editor at start-up publication BetaKit *and director of communications at Sprouter, which was acquired by Postmedia in 2011. Erin is also a speaker, writes a monthly column for the* Financial Post, *and is a tech commentator on* CTV News. *She has appeared in publications including* The New York Times, Forbes, CNN, *and* Canadian Business *and was named one of* Marketing Magazine's *top 30 Under 30 marketers. Her claim to fame is being retweeted by Oprah—twice.*
(Highlights from our interview, recorded July 6, 2023.)

WILLFUL IS AN ONLINE ESTATE planning platform, a company I run with my husband, Kevin. I never thought I would be in the estate planning business, but a personal experience with a loved one passing away highlighted the barriers to access. Together, we built a platform to make the process more accessible and easy. I've run my own businesses and been involved in the start-up space for a long time. I consider myself a terrible employee and lifelong entrepreneur. Most of the credit goes to Kevin because he had the idea for the company. I was running a tech marketing agency at the time, working with funded start-ups and companies like PayPal and Telus.

Kevin didn't have fundamental coding skills or an MBA to get him off the ground, so we began by building an advisory network around him to add expertise. The company launched in October 2017, and it was about a year before I came on and we hired our first full-time employee.

Recently, we used Working Genius, an assessment tool to find the areas of work you gravitate toward and love, and Kevin was the inventor and galvanizer. Being a galvanizer is crucial to leadership, especially in the early stages of a start-up. A galvanizer is a person who builds excitement and consensus around an idea, and to me, that perfectly encapsulates what helped get Willful off the ground. Being a galvanizer meant when we called a lawyer for help drafting legal documents, Kevin could convince them he was worth listening to. Founders galvanize around a mission, and we're passionate about the mission behind Willful: to ensure every Canadian has a solid estate plan, help Canadian families avoid what we went through, make it affordable, and increase access to justice. Every time we do an interview or hire, we return to the why behind it all. This helps people resonate with the idea, create an emotional connection with what we're doing, and build trust.

A founder has to be able to do it all. You don't have staff or departments; you have to be the janitor, the finance person, HR, and a little bit of everything. As Willful gained traction, Kevin needed operational experience, and I joined as CEO. We hired our CTO, Matt, who's been with us for four years now, to take over technology and build the platform. We use a framework called Entrepreneur Operating System, which has an accountability chart like an org chart but without names; it maps out functions. If there is a function without a person to fill it, then we decide if we should hire someone to fill that function. In the early days, for example, we needed people to know about our products, so we hired a marketing person. We needed someone to answer customer questions, so we hired a customer support person.

When I worked at my first start-up for Sarah Prevette, she created a culture of autonomy where I could shape my workday. She gave me freedom, flexibility, and trust, and in exchange, I gave her more of myself than I ever would have to another employer because I wanted to make a difference and do a great job for her. The experience stuck with me, especially when juxtaposed against my next workplace, which was the opposite; I was treated like a number, without empathy or common sense. When I went to Willful, I swore I would work to create a culture where people are treated like adults. If I can't think of a good reason to say no, I don't. I'm open to suggestions, and most importantly, I care about people beyond being a number in the company.

Our overarching strategy and trajectory is not growth at all costs: to take tens of millions in VC funding, have to triple in size every year, burn people out, and replace them until they burn out again. Even before having kids, I didn't want to be someone who was working 24/7. I hated hustle culture, working until two in the morning, sleeping four hours, and having a smoothie for every meal because you don't have time for a lunch break. When you're an entrepreneur, you can design what work looks like. Part of that is a social contract where I say, "Here is what it is going to feel like to work here." I realized how valuable it was to have people committed to the Willful mission like I had been committed to Sarah. Managing our growth trajectory means we're growing a lot but not at the pace of a unicorn or dictated by venture capitalist expectations.

When we raised investment in 2020, I called one of the investors after we closed. I had seen enough movies to know if I didn't grow the company, the board would kick me out in three years, so I wanted to stay ahead of the curve. "What should I be doing? What courses should I take? What books should I read?" He told me I was the first to ask him those questions, and I thought a lot about that. Was it because I was a female founder? Many people have arrogance/confidence that makes them believe they'll never be obsolete, whereas I want to soak everything up and learn. I don't have an MBA and never plan to get one; I'm never going to be one of those people on their Peloton, reading seven business books—give yourself permission not to do what all these other people are doing.

There's a benefit to running a company with my husband because we can share the deepest, darkest days with each other. But also, our job is outward-facing to inspire confidence. To be transparent, it's not always a rosy Mary Poppins picture. Companies go through ups and downs, and it would be a disservice to paint everything with rose gold and pretend everything is always okay. We are committed to transparency but with an understanding that our role as leaders is to inspire confidence and trust. Entrepreneurship is the ultimate gift of flexibility—you set the policies and the approach. There's also a lot of sacrifice; you can't just turn off and go home for the night, and it's a roller coaster. As someone who tries to convince everyone to quit their job and be an entrepreneur, my advice is to do it. The worst-case scenario is that it doesn't work out, and you get another job. But, you're smart, and so that'll be easy.

43

Leadership Resilience

Stacey Copas lives in Sydney, Australia, where she is the founder of the Academy of Resilience and author of How to Be Resilient. *She works with organizations who want their people to be more engaged and productive, teaching others to grow through challenge, adversity, and uncertainty, rather than just go through it.*
                    (Highlights from our interview, recorded June 23, 2023.)

MANY LEADERS HAVE FOUND THEIR go-to methods to motivate and equip their teams aren't as effective in the age of hybrid working. I speak with them about resilience, not just their own, but how to develop, nurture, and build resilience in the people around them. My perspective on resilience in a business context isn't about coping. Coping is reactive, and resilience is a proactive tool you can build through daily and regular rituals. With leaders, the starting point is communication; they need consistent, informal communication with the people they work with. Too often, leadership is seen as hierarchical, where leaders are at least one step removed from a business's day-to-day. I encourage leaders to start with small conversations and grow from there; you build trust, and people feel more confident and are open and honest. Communication is the starting point, and then looking for the bright spots and helping others look for the bright spots. To motivate others, you have to understand what inspires, drives, and motivates them, and these can be different for everybody.

People think uncertainty is negative, but when nothing is certain, anything is possible. I help people see uncertainty as a blank canvas, as infinite possibility. Uncertainty is an opportunity; it's a creative process you can drive. You're never on a plateau; you're either moving forward or backward. You can move forward by leaning into curiosity, seeing the blank canvas, and creating whatever you want. When I talk about transformation, I go back to my own journey. I had an accident at 12 that left me a quadriplegic. I was going to be a vet, had everything lined up ahead of me, and had to go back to square one. Three years ago, COVID hit, and my business and identity as a keynote speaker were suddenly gone. Slowly, I found new ways to support people through online conversations. I had to realize this was an opportunity. Yes, it was a challenge, but I found I could create a greater sense of intimacy and relationship with an audience virtually. I reached a much broader audience and helped them completely change how they view their businesses.

Sometimes, people think they must wait to be appointed a leader—but we're all leaders. We all have a center of influence; we just need to take it on. My advice for aspiring leaders is not to wait for someone to tap you on the shoulder and say you're a leader. Everyone's actions, behavior, and interactions lead and influence people, whether it's in a positive way or a not-so-positive way. Embrace that, and work to clarify what you want to transfer to other people. Then do what you need to do to nurture, develop, and encourage that; show up consistently and embrace being a leader as a privilege, not a pressure or burden. For me, that means I'm always learning and growing, seeing every aspect of my life as continuous improvement.

44

The Ingredients of Leadership

*Chef **Matt Basile** spent over a decade disrupting the food industry as the founder of Toronto's most recognizable food truck brand, Fidel Gastro's, and popular gastropub Lisa Marie. Today, as the cofounder of Alchemy Grills, he's taking on a new frontier—disrupting the barbecue and live-fire cooking landscape. In an industry steeped in tradition, Matt is always striving to do things differently. For two seasons, Matt hosted the reality television show* Rebel Without a Kitchen, *which aired on Netflix, Travel and Escape Channel, the Cooking Channel, and the Asian Food Channel. As a content creator, he also creates original content, including delicious recipes and grilling tips, which he shares on his YouTube channel. Matt and his partner, Kyla Zanardi, are also the best-selling authors of two cookbooks:* Street Food Diaries *and* Brunch Life.*
(Highlights from our interview, recorded August 11, 2023.)*

YEARS AGO, I WAS WORKING in advertising as a writer but never felt connected to my work; I wanted to start my own company. The only thing I knew how to do was cook, so I came up with a business plan for Fidel Gastro's, a Cuban sandwich restaurant, and presented it to the bank for funding. Long story short, that didn't work out. I was ready to walk away when someone asked me to cook one night at a party, and something amazing happened—the whole energy of the party shifted toward me cooking food, which became like an extension of the party. This was an interesting business model. I wouldn't need a fixed location; I'd be a sandwich DJ who rolls into events. There wasn't a formula to rely on; I had to use my intuition, creative thinking, and work ethic to see it through. We did our first pop-up, which was incredibly successful, and used that momentum and social media to build a following. As a natural evolution from the pop-up, we got a food truck, and I started filming a reality TV show about these experiences. All the momentum led to me signing a lease to a full-service restaurant.

Up to that point, I had trusted my gut to make decisions, but opening a restaurant was something I was "supposed" to do because that's what people did, right? Luckily, it was popular because I was the worst boss anyone could have back then. I was loud and short-tempered, running on no sleep with a camera in my face. I was more concerned with the optics of what was happening versus the nitty-gritty business behind the scenes. I was doing a lot of things but proficient in none of them, and I didn't teach or nurture; there was no inspiration there. About three years into owning the restaurant, I traveled to Southeast Asia for work and was gone for a month, with a 12-hour time difference. Giving others responsibility in my absence made me change how I worked, hired, and trained. I had to become a leader and find my own voice and style. We established a team, and despite having multiple things on the go, I learned to approach each layer differently, prioritize my time, and support talent in others. No matter the format, whether you are the captain of a sports team or a manager at McDonald's, leaders always communicate best from a place of understanding. You have to appreciate everyone's job and contribution. Working in the dish pit is tough and definitely not glamorous; I know because I did it for years in my parent's basement, but without it, nothing happens—you can't just eat off your hands. As a leader, the more you've done yourself, the better you can coach others and see all jobs as important. If the dish pit falls apart, everything crumbles.

Hospitality is about creating work and business that revolve around making others feel good, whether you create a product or moments for people to take away. Does it cost money, time, and energy? Yes. However, in exchange, you create joy. Alchemy Grills is my first product company; with it, I bring the concept of hospitality to a non-hospitality-based industry. As the creative firestarter, I manage all things culinary, community- and content marketing–focused. I develop secondary and tertiary products and work with engineers to ensure we make barbecues people want to put in their backyards and love to use. No matter what aspect I'm working on, it's important to understand when to take the reins and when to listen. The best parts of Alchemy have been moments where I'm not the expert and bring back new knowledge I can apply to other aspects of the business.

I worked hands-on with engineers in Guangzhou, China, during manufacturing. They knew how to develop prototypes, and I brought applicable knowledge important to a user. I may never be the smartest person in the room, but I value my perspective and my team's. Offering a perspective rooted in knowledge, applied in a specific way, is incredibly valuable. When I traveled to see the prototypes, I explained that the best way to test them was to use them. We couldn't fire them up on the manufacturing floor, so I set up shop outside and started making food for everyone at the factory. At the end of the day, I got to speak to about 70 people. They shared what they wanted next, so I made smoked mussels, curry sauces, and barbecued fried rice. I cooked for four days, and day by day, people started engaging with me more. This was the first time anyone who'd visited the factory had cooked them lunch. The relationships established during that trip allowed us to get our production run done, shipped, packed, and approved with a five-week turnaround, which is almost unheard of.

There is a quote about never doing what you're most passionate about; you should find something you're good at and spend time getting great at it. And honestly, I fundamentally disagree with that. Passion is incredibly important because you'll only get from good to great with passion. The journey can be long; sometimes, it's six months, sometimes 20 years. With passion, you achieve greatness faster, more efficiently, and with a smile. It is passion that others recognize in you that makes them want to be part of building a community with you. Passion is business minded; it's why people buy from us and what drove Alchemy Grills' production. Whether people recognize it or not, they buy a grill from Alchemy because of passion.

45

Leadership and Communication

I'M **ALISON STRATTEN,** AND I'M not sure I need an intro in this context, but here you go. I'm a parent, a writer, a student, and cocreator at UnMarketing. Growing up, my mom would leave clippings from the *New York Times* with my breakfast. Articles and photos about things I was interested in, music or fashion, a new movie or book she thought I might like. Something to read with my toast and orange slices. I never really thought about it that much. Sometimes I would read them, sometimes I wouldn't. You know how kids are.

It wasn't until I got older and became a parent that I understood what she was doing.

She worked hard; days at TD Bank, evenings and weekends teaching piano lessons (her holiday concerts were legendary), so we didn't always have time for breakfast together. She filled our house with classical music, Dickens and Bronte novels, but gave me articles about Alanis's new album, modern art exhibits and poetry, book reviews on women authors, unions, protests, and articles about the dangers of smoking among other things teens do (don't judge me. . .).

She never told me what she thought right away; she left me the article. She always knew what I was into, or going through, and she showed me one clipping at a time, guiding me, in the way she knew I would listen. Sometimes, artists grow up in homes where there is always paint, clay, and space to make a mess, authors in homes filled with books, and musicians in places filled with singing. Leadership can be unseen labor, the kind that provides scaffolding, opportunity, and access, and leadership is communicating in a way that we can hear. My mom taught me what she cared about and about the world, in the way she knew I'd listen and learn.

In business we are often told that leaders have "strong communication skills," but what does that actually mean? We tend to focus on ways to craft a perfect message for everyone—our market, potential market, employees, and teams. But communication is a relational skill—there is no perfect message, and the right messages are only available to use when we've developed both self-awareness and connection with those we're trying to reach. Leaders focus on storytelling, on sharing their ideas and building strong teams. Their ability to make their vision clear is paramount, as is their ability to translate this vision to others and have it stick. Stickiness isn't about perfection—in the age of disruption, particularly with advancements in AI, authentic messages break through the noise.

46

Leadership Is Telling the Right Story

*With over a decade of experience, **Derek Schoen** is a seasoned leader in the world of marketing and team management. Currently overseeing advertising and social media strategy within the hospitality sector, he is known for a relentless pursuit of innovation and creating healthy work environments.*
(Highlights from our interview, recorded May 22, 2023.)

I'VE BUILT MY CAREER ON innovation, trying new things, and seeing if we can see them through. For a leader, risk-taking means being willing to put yourself out there and accept, loudly and vocally, when innovation works and doesn't. Follow-through is the key. Many people with great ideas throw them out in a meeting and walk away without concern for the mess they've left. To be a leader, you have to be ready to put in the hard work, follow through, and build a team. You need to be ready to see the idea through to the next step and deliver on innovation.

A leader has to be willing to fight for the resources needed and invest in their team's professional growth and development. Otherwise, they are heading for burnout. I'm a marketer, first and foremost. Even when communicating internally, it's marketing, selling the right story to the right leader to get the resources I need for my team. Our CCO, CFO, and CEO each have their own take on the business they run. I have to tell the right story, bring up relevant points and how we're impacting their piece of the business. You have to understand the approval path—who is the true person or people with the final say in what you're trying to do? If you walk into a room full of leaders and don't already know the answer to the question you're asking, you are probably in trouble. By building understanding and consensus over time, you can more easily convince and convert senior decision-makers. All of this requires awareness. Who are the decision-makers in my path? Who are the detractors, the neutrals, and the advocates in the room?

I moved into a VP position two years ago, and the most important thing I did when I got in there was to sit down with other senior leaders and ask about their impressions of our department. Overall, the most significant negative I heard was a lack of transparency. And so, for the next 12 months, in every decision I made, I thought, "How does this impact the narrative we are looking to change around transparency?" Am I saying no to doing a report because it's too much work? Have I shared enough numbers, and am I trying to make something look good when we should be more honest? I knew it was vital that every decision we made went toward that narrative because it stood in the way of our goals. We updated the way we do reporting and our meeting cadences. We did training to let others in the company learn more about what we did and built trust. It took time and was a multistep process, but when we got our interdepartmental feedback last year, one of the highlights was that we are viewed as transparent.

Especially in creative spaces, you have to be able to separate yourself from the work and not take feedback personally. Most people who give feedback are there for a reason and are working to achieve the same overall goals as you. Understanding where they are coming from will only help you get better. As a young leader, the biggest lesson I learned was the value of ongoing feedback, the little touch points that help keep your team on the right track. However, I've also learned that this only works for some. I had a team member who did not react well to ongoing feedback, and with them, I developed a process where, twice a year, we built out a growth plan that talks about three main themes we want to work on. Most importantly, the growth plan includes a section on how I will be helping along the way with support and resources. Using themes in our goal-setting has been incredibly successful. You have to be flexible. You cannot expect your leadership to be perfect for everyone. It is also important to me that people feel supported and cared for when they leave. Don't burn bridges while you build because the more allies you have, the better. Creating relationships and teams whenever you can builds a reputation around you as someone trustworthy. You find better opportunities and have others vouching for you and your work, and it softens the blow when you make a mistake.

My goal is to never stop learning and to stay on the cutting edge. The communication world is ever-changing, especially on the digital front. The last few years have brought us tough times in Las Vegas. When a mass tragedy happens in such a tight-knit community, as a leader, sometimes you have to compartmentalize what you're feeling personally, take a deep breath, and focus on how to manage your team first. If you can't do that as a leader, it's better to be honest and step away and ask for help. You have to understand your own limits. At the end of the day, it doesn't matter what level of a company you are in; understanding who you are and your capabilities and capacities is incredibly important. Whether it's a time of personal crisis, community crisis, or company crisis, you've got to make sure that you're watching everybody's energy levels and that they're OK to be at work that day. And, if they insist on being there, take some things off their plate. Leadership is about grace, empathy, and vulnerability. In a crisis, you have to be able to give people grace and change your margin of error.

Leaders can come from anywhere. I guarantee you there are leaders on every person's team who go unnoticed. They are the canary in the coal mine, the cheerleader in the background, and keeping your team together. It is important to identify those people, empower them, and listen to them because their feedback is often the most valuable in the room. Leadership isn't a one-person thing. It's all about building a team of leaders who bring the whole place along.

47

Mostly Money Leadership

Preet Banerjee is a consultant to the wealth management industry, specializing in commercial applications of behavioral finance. He is the founder of MoneyGaps, an investor and personal finance educator. Preet hosts the Mostly Money podcast, where he helps listeners take control of their finances by exploring the full world of all things money with expert interviews.
(Highlights from our interview, recorded May 30, 2023.)

WHY DO PEOPLE MAKE BAD decisions about money? The first generation of behavioral finance and economics assume people were rational actors making self-serving decisions. When we tried to understand money mistakes, we chalked it up to people being irrational. That was a weird assumption to make, though, because when we look around, a lot of people are being irrational. Instead, people are predictably irrational. They repeatedly make the same kinds of money mistakes, and there are patterns. The current thinking is that we should look at the things people value. Maybe they don't value money more than status, for example, and this shapes their spending. It's not that they are irrational; instead, they look at the world from a different perspective, a bigger perspective than just money. Behavioral finance asks, "We know we need to save more than we spend to save money. Why do we have so much trouble doing that?"

Personal finance success is 90% psychology and 8% math. The missing 2% is a testament to how unimportant the math is. It really has nothing to do with numbers; it's about emotions and psychology. I was called to this work because I made significant money mistakes when I was younger. I graduated from university with no money, but instead of getting a real job, I went to racing school to become a professional race car driver. I got my first credit card at the Toronto Indy because it had a picture of my favorite race car driver on it. No one had taught me how to use credit, so I quickly racked up a ton of debt. There I was—graduated, back in school without an income and with my credit card, commuting an hour and a half and eating crackers for breakfast, lunch, and dinner. I kept getting deeper and deeper into debt; it was a constant level of stress. I became passionate about personal finance to abandon that anxiety and learned everything I could. When my auto racing career ended, because I ran out of money and talent, I went to work as a financial services advisor. The people I met had different challenges about money, and I felt I could make a difference by sharing what I knew. I knew there were people like me who just needed to be taught the basics to make a significant difference in their lives.

There is so much financial information out there, more than ever before. When sensational headlines come along, all of a sudden, you get nervous. There are so many voices and opinions of varying levels of credibility that it becomes impossible to stay the course or make informed changes. Someone is a fitness expert and is now sharing their opinion about Bitcoin. We saw this, especially with cryptocurrencies and NFTs. Many people with very limited knowledge of corporate and personal finance suddenly had coins to sell and affiliate links to trading platforms. And a lot of them made money, so we have this entire generation whose first step into investing was incredibly risky. I wouldn't even call them investments; they were the riskiest speculations we've ever seen. That's a horrible way to get started because that's the reference point for the rest of their investing lives. My work may get fewer eyeballs than a sensational hot take, but I try to be a calming voice and present facts so people can make informed decisions.

I've always been attracted to school and learning and recently completed my doctorate of business administration. It's a PhD for professionals, allowing you to apply academic rigor to a problem you're seeing in the professional world. My years in the industry, personal experiences, and those of my clients informed my question and direction: What advice do you give to someone who doesn't have a million dollars and is looking for a financial advisor? It is a pretty important question not to have an answer for—most people don't have a million dollars. Financial services are corporations designed to maximize value for their shareholders first and clients second. When you have a lot of money, you have a lot of choices between good advice options. But until you get to that point, you're on your own. I would argue this is when people are most teachable, when they don't have wealth yet but show signs of the potential for having wealth. I shifted my focus to a different part of the wealth spectrum because that's where there was an absence of resources and leadership.

For the average person, going to the financial advisor is a lot like going to the dentist. They know they should go but aren't looking forward to it. Not everyone is a numbers person. Most people also need similar solutions: you've got dependents, you need insurance, you're self-employed, you need disability insurance, etc. You can create a model that can scale to deal with the mass market, which requires high volume, light touch. MoneyGaps was designed to give people a one-page financial report card and an overall grade point average. This provides a picture of how they are doing compared with other people like them. MoneyGaps was designed to be radically simple.

Growing up, a staple was watching *The National* with my parents. Peter Mansbridge is an iconic figure for many reasons—the voice, the authority, the calmness. Whether content creation or education assets, his work and style have been my example in my work, presenting challenging information in a calm, confident way that emboldens trust and credibility with the audience. When he was a guest on my podcast, I had to be cool when the whole time I was thinking, "I am interviewing PETER MANSBRIDGE." Even though there's no planet upon which we'd be considered equals, he made me feel that way. There is a tendency for people to withdraw and look for someone else to take the lead, but true leadership is about stepping up to the plate and presenting information in an accessible, trustworthy way. It doesn't have to come from a Canadian journalism icon, a CEO, or a board chair—a leader can be anyone who can galvanize others behind a value. You have to know yourself, your values, and what you're fighting for.

48

Leadership and Education

DR. MAYDIANNE ANDRADE IS A professor of biological sciences at the University of Toronto Scarborough. For the last 15 years, she has done extensive research on knowledge translation with respect to equity in the workplace and academic contexts. She is the founder and current cochair of the Toronto Initiative for Diversity and Equity (TIDE) and cofounder and president of the Canadian Black Scientist Network (CBSN), a national organization aimed at increasing the visibility and inclusion of Black people in STEM in Canada. Maydianne also served as vice dean of faculty affairs and equity, which supports faculty across 15 departments at the University of Toronto Scarborough, from recruitment through retirement, and acting dean for six months.

Alison had the opportunity to sit down with Maydianne, who shared that TIDE arose from her personal experience in academia; in 23 years, she had never had a Black colleague in the sciences. She began looking at the literature on equitable representation and unconscious bias. She found that a major review of the literature on university practices in Canada and the United States offered two critical findings: the importance of engaged leadership and policy and that those on the ground enacting policies need to be more educated on their goals and how to implement policy equitably. Most institutions had staff who did equity or brought in specialists. However, these individuals had no experience on the ground. The report was clear—they needed peer-to-peer, faculty-led education and workshops.

Since its founding, TIDE has engaged thousands across the university and created online education modules to complement their work. Maydianne said, "The key pieces in founding TIDE were recognizing the problem and finding literature with effective solutions." In leadership, it is essential to ensure there is evidence you can use to justify your planning, to show that your work is efficacious and that there is uptake. "Those of us who are Black academics in Canada, especially in the sciences, have recognized for many years that we are underrepresented. One part of the problem is issues with the education pipeline; we have evidence that Black students are streamed out of fields that make them eligible for university. Beyond that, we see Black people's experiences causing them to leave the field or have difficulty getting a job, which is aligned with what we expect from the literature on bias. After George Floyd's murder and conversations across the country, a group of us knew we had to do something. We decided to create the Canadian Black Scientist Network to support one another."

At the time of founding, Maydianne had been a program administrator and organized conferences, so she took the lead. When we spoke, Maydianne shared that it was clear right away how engaged everyone was: "With little visibility of Black academics, young people did not see science as a field they could enter. We knew that if we could make a name for ourselves nationally, we could draw in more people and be visible role models for young people. We also could serve in consultation roles for universities, the government, and other organizations when needed. An individual within an institution does not have much power, but if you are part of a national network, you have a much stronger voice." Their first meeting had 24 people; now, they have over 700 members internationally and held their first conference in 2022. With TIDE and CBSN, Maydianne shared that they are now focused on stabilization. One of the issues with the work is that they have many volunteers and constantly have to apply for grants. When they apply for money for their mentorship program, they include programming for a youth science fair and wrap in administrative support for the network. Grant applications are a lot of work, which makes it challenging to get other things done. They recently convinced two major granting agencies to provide sustained funding over the next few years. With that, they are opening up more space for panel and policy discussions and lobbying the government. Currently, their focus is getting others to step up and do leadership work. Not everyone wants to take a leadership role, but many have the skills and are never allowed opportunities to lead.

According to what we see from large consultancy firms such as McKinsey and Boston Consulting Group, equity principles in the workplace are table stakes for leaders now. They can no longer be left to HR; you have to be trying and, at the very least, understand the vocabulary. The literature is crystal clear—diverse teams do better than non-diverse teams. You are undercutting your bottom line by not getting on board. If you lack expertise or experience, find a consultant, work with your local business association to bring in experts, or pool your resources with other entrepreneurs. Be honest and transparent and listen to your employees when issues surface because ignoring them will not help. Maydianne advises aspiring leaders to "be authentic, know the type of person you are, and not be afraid to share yourself, your passions and aspirations with your organization. Think about what you want to accomplish in terms of goals rather than titles or promotions."

49

Gaming Leadership

David G. Schwartz, a gaming historian, professor, and the associate vice provost for faculty affairs at the University of Nevada, Las Vegas, studies gambling and casinos, video games, popular culture, Las Vegas, tourism, and higher education. Dave has written several books (which are some of Scott's favorites), including At the Sands, Grandissimo: The First Emperor of Las Vegas, Roll the Bones: The History of Gambling, *and* Boardwalk Playground: The Making, Unmaking, & Remaking of Atlantic City. *Born in Atlantic City, New Jersey, David earned his bachelor's degree (a double major in anthropology and history) as well as his master's degree from the University of Pennsylvania before receiving his doctorate in US history from UCLA. His academic interest in gambling stems from his hands-on experience in the casino industry as a security officer, surveillance officer, and Mr. Peanut.*

(Highlights from our interview, recorded July 6, 2023.)

As OMBUDS, I HELP PEOPLE resolve conflicts informally, as opposed to going through HR or formal channels, which often entails asking folks to better listen to and understand each other. Many people I work with have transactional concerns; maybe they're doing work outside their classification and want to be reclassified. Some of the work is relational, where people want to interact with one another better, and some is organization, for example, helping people navigate tenure. In addition to one-on-one work, I lead workshops on a range of communication and conflict resolution topics. We also have a mediation practice that helps facilitate conversations between people.

Kenneth Thomas and Ralph Kilmann's famous study of conflict styles relates that people handle conflict in one of five ways: they avoid (satisfy neither their needs nor anyone else's), accommodate (help the others at their own expense), compete (seek to satisfy their own wants at the expense of others), compromise (basically split things down the middle), or collaborate (everyone shares ideas and work together to find a solution). As a leader, avoiding conflict is the worst thing you can do, hands down. Most people would rather hear any news, positive or negative, than radio silence; leaders need to turn conflict from destructive to productive. In general, it's best to communicate often and let people know what's happening. And it goes both ways: the best leaders listen and solicit feedback from everyone. Even if you don't like what you're hearing, the simple fact that you're hearing it is usually appreciated.

I used to study gambling history, and there are some good examples there. Bugsy Siegel was an awful leader; he didn't listen to the experts or his customers. He was in it for himself. It's fascinating because he has such a reputation, but if you look at what he actually did, he was an awful leader who made everyone around him angry. There was so much to go around—there really shouldn't have been anything to argue about, but he was driven by ego. We can also see how leaders respond to the structures around them. Until the 1960s, the casino industry was like a mom-and-pop business in many ways, although it was an unsavory mom-and-pop. Gamblers put together enough money to buy a casino. They knew the business, and they knew their customers. In the 1970s, with the transition to publicly traded companies, we saw professionalization. Leadership became incentivized to return value to shareholders over everything else, including building relationships with customers or employees. And they had to deliver shareholder value, or they'd be sued; the structure was set up so that they couldn't do business the old ways. But what if we change that structure? If you did, you would have an environment responsive to customers. For example, you have Derek Stevens, who owns several casinos, including Circa, Downtown. When Derek came into the business, he spent a lot of time in the casino, watching customers to see what they were doing. And he's a gambler himself. To this day, if you go to Stadium Swim or the huge sportsbook in Circa, you can see Derek there, watching or betting on sports. You can go to the Long Bar at the D and have a drink with him. When many other places are owned by real estate investment trusts, having an authentic connection cannot be duplicated. In any business, those with passion and authenticity, who listen and make themselves accessible, go far.

Communication is going to become even more important with AI. Words, as themselves, are becoming meaningless in that you can ask AI a question, and it will give you a (hopefully) technically correct but recycled answer. We can communicate in so many ways, and we're saying less and less. It's uncommunication. Uncommunication has a long history in politics. For example, someone says, "We are going to change welfare as we know it." If you don't like welfare, that means we're going to get rid of it, but if you do like it, you might hear that we're going to have more of it. Now it's invading all kinds of speech. In this context, authenticity is very important. People aren't interested in perfect communication; they want something heartfelt that says something and means it.

If you look at professors' online forums, many feel that the level of preparation isn't what it used to be. Right or wrong, the point is to teach the students we have. Leaders need to work with the people you have, not the ones you wish you had. A lot of that is meeting people where they are, giving scaffolding where needed. And listen. Every day as ombuds, when people come to see me, I'm the dumbest person in the room. I know much less about their specialties, and that's humbling and stimulating at the same time. I learn every day. But authenticity is the heart of it all. Growing up, the first academic professor type I saw was Carl Sagan in *Cosmos*. He had this sonorous, deep, calm voice and made everything seem so interesting. But I can't talk like that; I get excited about something and talk quickly. If I can't connect to the crowd by projecting gravitas, I can spark their interest with my enthusiasm because that's me, being myself. Everyone has an authentic mode, and it shows. Embrace it.

50

A Note about Burnout

BURNOUT SEEMS TO BE EVERYWHERE, no matter the industry, whether you are an entrepreneur, CEO, or anywhere in between. Burnout is work-related stress, "a state of physical or emotional exhaustion that also involves a sense of reduced accomplishment and loss of personal identity" (Mayo Clinic 2021). A 2022 survey conducted by Asana of 10,000 knowledge workers in seven countries found that 70% of people experienced burnout in the last year, with 40% of workers believing burnout to be an inevitable part of success (Asana 2022). Other data showed gender and age gaps on the issue of burnout, with women reporting more burnout than their male counterparts and younger workers more likely to experience burnout than older workers. Over the last few years, even as many companies have earned record profits with remote and hybrid workforces, some have become obsessed with productivity and presenteeism. A 2023 Slack survey of over 18,000 desk workers, managers, and executives revealed that 71% of business leaders say they are under pressure to squeeze more productivity out of the workers. Most measure productivity in traditional ways, even though work has changed, talking during meetings or answering emails quickly, for example. At the same time, worker engagement is low, and rates of burnout are high (Slack 2023).

Deloitte partnered with Workplace Intelligence to survey 2100 employees and C-level executives in the United States, United Kingdom, Canada, and Australia to look at ways leaders could improve their employees' and their own well-being. The report found that 70% of C-suite respondents reported were seriously considering quitting their job for one that better supports their well-being. Not only are these executives struggling with their own challenges, but they are significantly overestimating how well their employees are doing and how supported they feel by their leaders. "Many employees don't feel that their executives have been supportive during the pandemic—but the C-suite sees things much differently. For example, only 47% of workers believe their executives understand how difficult the pandemic has been for them, yet 90% of the C-suite say they *do* recognize how challenging it's been. Similarly, while only 53% of employees feel that their company's executives have been making the best decisions for their well-being during the pandemic, 88% of the C-suite believe their decision-making has been exemplary" (Hatfield et al. 2022).

There is clearly a gap, and leadership is the key to closing it; workplaces that foster flexibility report lower burnout and higher scores for productivity, connection, and company culture. Rather than disconnection, remote and hybrid workers have been shown to feel more connected to their manager and company values and equally or more connected to their teams than fully in-person employees. When evaluating company culture, flexible and remote work policies were named as the number one factor in improving employee experience (Future Forum 2023). Deloitte's study pointed to the value of health-savvy CEO's: those who appreciate that "decisions relating to health and health care can have a significant impact on the culture of the organization, the way in which work gets done, the cascading effects of that work in spaces and places beyond the organization's four walls, and the power of the CEO's personal brand to support people's health." These are leaders who understand drivers of health and that matters of health drive organizational culture, trust, and brand (Abrams et al. 2021).

Sixty-eight percent of employees and 81% of the C-suite say improving their well-being is more important than advancing their career; addressing burnout is no longer an option. Burnout isn't a simple problem, and it won't have a simple solution; it requires awareness and connection, communication and flexibility; leadership that understands companies are made up of people, and people thrive in environments where they can create meaning, experience belonging, and are given opportunities for leadership and collaboration. To learn more about burnout, we spoke to expert Dr. Susan Biali Haas; you'll find her in the following chapter. We encourage you to read her story and consider the impact burnout is having on you, your leadership, and your workforce.

51

Leadership's Greatest Challenge

Dr. Susan Biali Haas MD is a medical doctor and passionate mental health educator with a focus on burnout prevention. Her work aims to reduce stigma around mental health, encourage conversation, and change the way we think about work and life.

(Highlights from our interview, recorded June 29, 2023.)

OVER THE LAST FEW YEARS, it has been heartening to see the explosion of interest from organizations in mental health and, particularly, the well-being of their employees. Today, neuroscience, physiology, and the science of high performance teach us that our best performance, our greatest impact, comes from a balance—of strategically pacing ourselves and taking care of ourselves in intentional ways. As a student and doctor, I slogged and worked hard my entire life. I got away with it through school, university, and even medical school. However, when I got to residency training, with 36-hour shifts, sleep deprivation, and untreated trauma, I had no tools or support. My emergency medicine residency left me with burnout, depression, and trauma. Although I practiced primary care medicine for 20 years, I wanted to educate and empower people around preventative medicine, mental health, well-being, and work.

189

I was frustrated with only being able to spend 10 or 15 minutes with each patient. I wanted to make a bigger impact—I had all the knowledge and training but needed more time. I knew if I had time to talk with patients about their whole lives, their health problems would improve.

Coaching represented a way for me to work with people deeply in their lives. At the time, life coaching was emerging, and I saw this as a construct within which I could have more time than medicine. Today, there are courses at Harvard Medical School around lifestyle medicine and coaching, which is wonderful to see. Often, when I share my burnout experience, people have a moment of awakening and realization of how lost they've gotten in the pursuit of success. I share clinical symptoms of burnout, and they realize what they've been doing isn't sustainable. Once that realization happens, I work to equip them with insights, tools, and strategies related to their work, body, mind, and psychology. My three-part transformation model implements insights, tools, and strategies related to work, psychology, and evidence-based medical science/neuroscience. The work piece is central to the process; we work at transforming their choices, and they completely transform their lives.

Foundational research on workplace mental health and burnout outlines six areas that drive burnout in an organization. Burnout is a considerable risk if these challenges are left unaddressed and unacknowledged:

Work overload: Leaders need to understand processes and workflow issues and work to ensure we aren't demanding unreasonable things.

Lack of control: Workers lack control and agency; the more control and agency you give creatively, the more resilient your organization will be against burnout.

Insufficient rewards: Lack of recognition, lack of feeling valued or appreciated; this begins with fairness around pay and then showing appreciation and communicating value. Simply thanking people for work well done and recognizing contributions profoundly shapes people's resilience and prevents burnout. I encourage leaders to build meaningful recognition, which is about two-way conversation; you must understand what meaningful rewards are to your team.

Workplace community issues: Lack of psychological safety and belonging. Toxic workplace practices such as bullying cannot be tolerated. Belonging is a huge part of our resilience as human beings and burnout prevention. Again, this has to be intentional and meaningful to the team.

Values conflicts: Lastly, there needs to be more understanding; workers must feel heard and supported through challenging times. In health care, for example, we often witness suffering and are powerless to help because of systemic issues.

As my career has morphed through medicine, coaching, and now big-picture mental health and burnout work with organizations and leaders, the responsibility of that platform is not lost on me. There is a balance between honoring those who hired me and supporting the people who trust me with their experiences; real sobriety comes with that. When I wrote my first book in 2008, an advisor told me no one would ever want to read a book about depression. It was probably the worst advice I've ever taken. While I included my depression story, I ignored my instincts and made it more upbeat and less authentic. Looking back, it highlights how little people talked about mental health then. But also, it's been a good lesson for me in trusting my instincts. It takes guts to be vulnerable and ahead of the curve, and I'm working to return to that.

First and foremost, I practice everything I teach, so it comes from a deep personal experience. I love a challenge, and my ultimate challenge was against burnout, depression, and trauma. I focus on what gives me life and helps me show up best for what I've been called to do. I have a mindfulness or spiritual prayer practice. I do a lot of journaling. I'm intentional about maintaining my close relationships. I have my own coach and often also get counseling. I'm aware of my weaknesses and am always working on my boundaries. I'm also very introverted, and introverts are at increased risk for burnout compared to extroverts; they also make up about 20%–30% of high-level business leaders. For those who want to do big things and are introverts, it's important to understand those parts of yourself and find ways for solo time. This isn't being selfish—it's essential if you want to have a sustainable impact on the world. One of the best things a leader can do is allow flexibility so people can have space to protect their energy. Imagine a space in which you can bring out the best for your company. How can we create environments that bring out the best in everybody?

52

UnLeadership and Transformations

UNLEADERSHIP IS ABOUT FOCUS, SEEING that within new strategies, technologies, and frameworks fighting for our attention lay the tried and true tenets of good business—because innovation is nothing but a bright and shiny new toy, unless it actually works. You can't fix bad service and poor products with a fancy new app. We live in a transformative time. The digital age has given us unlimited access to information and continues to create opportunities for emerging products and services we never thought possible. With all the excitement of our time comes confusion and fear for many businesses. Change can be daunting, and never have we lived in a time where change came so quickly.

Leading through change and transformation can be an enormous challenge. Successful organization change requires empathetic leadership only available to us through awareness and connection. Leaders need to anticipate how employees will react to change and have open communication and feedback. Unfortunately, that's rarely the case. According to a recent survey of over 200 leading executives, only half of those conducting a change effort have considered their team's sentiment about the change. Going on gut is not a strategy. You don't always need months of research; even a few conversations with key stakeholders can make a tremendous impact (Sanchez 2021).

Transformations require developing a sense of purpose or vision that guides decisions and shapes culture, repositioning your business and creating new areas of growth (Lancefield 2021). For leadership this means considering the impact on and needs and feelings of others, self-awareness, and mindfulness. Today's leaders need to rethink transformation as top-down and encourage self-leadership and leadership from all levels. Transformations require big thinking, tackling organization problems, and the courage to make difficult decisions and manage our own emotions. Through transformation, UnLeaders are those who make rough waters feel smooth, and related to trust and their ability to share vulnerability, they provide transparency and keep everyone working toward a shared vision.

53

Change Enthusiasm®

OUR WORLD IS BECOMING MORE VUCA (volatile, uncertain, complex, and ambiguous), right? So much going on, so much disruption, and the emotions are real and raw. Leading through change and transformation can be an enormous challenge. Successful organizational change requires empathetic leadership, which is only available through awareness, connection, and reflexivity. To learn more about leading through change we spoke to **Cassandra Worthy**, founder and CEO of Change Enthusiasm Global. A chemical engineer by training, Cassandra worked for giant Procter & Gamble before leaving corporate to help individuals and organizations flourish through change. According to McKinsey research, 70% of change projects fail to meet their intended goals, largely due to employee resistance and lack of management support (McKinsey & Company 2015). Cassandra and her workforce at Change Enthusiasm Global believe the true root cause of the resistance and lack of support manifests when organizations fail to acknowledge the biggest change adoption factor is their people *and* more importantly, the beliefs and emotions they embody. When your change plan focuses only on the business strategy, responsibilities, and timelines, it is missing your people's emotions and beliefs that power the change. Cassandra is on a mission to change that; her work is rooted in shifting the paradigm that emotions have no place in business, disrupting the idea that only logical, mind-led, stoic leaders should climb the ladder and become CEOs because they're level-headed. Change Enthusiasm Global creates value at the intersection of change and emotion, where they believe your growth potential is determined.

Decades ago, change management found its grounding within program management and was rooted in the concept of change being a linear thing, with a beginning, middle, and end. At Change Enthusiasm Global, they are charging forward a new frontier working in an area of practice they've dubbed the Change Growth Space. The Change Growth Space is rich with the mindset, the tools, and the skill sets that help individuals embrace the emotions they experience with change and use those emotions as a resource, energy, and fuel to move them through a challenge, embracing change as a means to grow and evolve. In today's world, change is no longer this simple, linear thing. Change is complex, often different type of changes layered on one another. We must deal with change in culture, business, and innovation and with customers, clients, employees, spouses, friends, and peers. Therefore, we need to arm ourselves and our people to navigate and grow through any change, to ultimately become better prepared for the next inevitable change, whether happening in our work or other aspects of our lives.

Change Enthusiasm® is a mindset best practiced in a culture with empathetic leadership, gratitude, and appreciation. Leaders create a courageous space where people feel safe being authentic and sharing genuine emotions. Cassandra works to empower the organization to practice the mindset, arming them with the tools to do it regularly, and then empowers and arms those responsible for energizing and influencing the organization with their own tool kit to allow that mindset to proliferate. Cassandra's passion for change is contagious. She wants to debunk the myth that emotions are to be left at the door of business. She says emotions should be our carry-ons because they exist regardless of whether you invite and acknowledge them. When you don't invite emotions, they can manifest in unproductive ways, such as venting, transferring energy, the downward spiral, the organizational churn, and attrition rates going through the roof. The Change Growth Space is about giving employees the means to create those courageous spaces and tools to share true emotions authentically and effectively. Their research found that 78% of working Americans more readily adapt to change when they feel safe sharing their truest emotions (Change Enthusiasm 2022). That data tells you to listen up and stop leaving emotion at the door of business. The leaders and organizations who embrace these concepts will make those who don't obsolete.

When Alison sat down with Cassandra, she shared her journey from the corporate world into entrepreneurship and thought leadership.

"Working in corporate, I always had a little whisper that there was something more I should be doing to make the world a better place, leveraging my unique talents and gifts. But I was having fun, solving complex problems, traveling the world, and creating connections working at Procter & Gamble, a huge, impressive company. I was learning so much, advancing in the company and advancing in my drinking career as well. Drinking quieted the whisper, the intuition, and I thought I could continue down the path, getting to the highest level possible, getting fatter paychecks, health benefits, a bigger house, and all that stuff. Both my parents are recovering alcoholics, and I used to go to AA meetings under the guise of supporting them to convince myself I wasn't like the other people in the room. I had convinced myself I couldn't be an alcoholic because I'd never been arrested for a DUI. And then, one night, I was arrested for a DUI. That was a moment of clarity, reality, devastation, pain, and guilt that led me to an awakening moment—I am an alcoholic, and that's OK. That inflection point within me that I am powerless over alcohol took my life on a completely different trajectory. I could no longer numb the whisper, and it got louder and louder. The whisper nurtured curiosity about what could be and grew into a shout, which one day landed me on stage, sharing the message of Change Enthusiasm. I had been practicing this mindset for years at that point, and seeing the impact of my energy coupled with this powerful message lit me up. In those moments, I knew this is my work."

For about two years, Cassandra grew her speaking business while leading an organization in corporate, basically doing two careers. She felt her life's energy pulling her in the direction of Change Enthusiasm®, but people weren't returning her phone calls, and her messages on LinkedIn weren't being responded to. It wasn't easy, but she shared how she rested on trust and belief in herself and her message. She created What-If Days: "What if I was a professional speaker, consultant, and thought leader running my own business? I would be working in a coffee shop, writing a blog post, or preparing for an interview." She created those days and wrote about them in her journal. Those seeds of inspiration kept her going, exploring her curiosity and leading her to where she is now. That trust got her her first paid speaking engagement, the second, and third, eventually leading to speaking full-time.

Cassandra believes we can lead from wherever we sit, even as individual contributors, without anyone reporting to us.

"I have met some of the most impactful influential leaders on the front lines: someone who runs one of the machines at a manufacturing facility, nurses, and frontline workers in health care. My definition of a leader is anyone with the power to influence another such that they want to follow, whether that be your behaviors, mindset, thoughts, or beliefs. I'll share some wisdom that my wife gave me permission to share. When we bring our flagship Change Growth Accelerator program to clients and speak to their leaders, they will often ask what tools they can give their team. They want to know what to give others to be prepared and enabled rather than focusing on themselves. They want to de-prioritize talking about developing their own awareness, fueled by the assumption that their skill set needs minimal work given they've already reached a high level in the organization. They just need their people to do what they're telling them to do. With her permission, I'll share my wife's advice: one of the best gifts you can give your team, organization, or workforce is a better, healthier, more emotionally self-aware you. When you do, you take care of your mind, body, heart, and spirit and show up better able to hold space, think more clearly, be in tune with your emotional energy, and recognize those same emotions in another. That is the leadership employees are hungry for today and into the future."

54

Transformative Leadership

Melissa Sargeant is CMO at AlphaSense, where she runs worldwide marketing initiatives including corporate and product branding, demand generation, product marketing, public relations, inbound sales development, and event management. Before AlphaSense, Melissa was CMO at email optimization leader Litmus, customer experience management disruptor SugarCRM, and e-commerce innovator ChannelAdvisor (ECOM). With more than 30 years of marketing experience in the tech sector, she has expertise in SaaS go-to-market strategy and execution, customer success, digital demand generation, and branding. Melissa also held senior marketing roles at Avalara, CA Technologies (Computer Associates), Digitalsmiths—A TiVo Company, Bluefire Security Technologies, and Guardent (VeriSign). Over the years Melissa has brought Scott in to speak to multiple audiences, most recently for AlphaSense in 2023.
(Highlights from our interview, recorded May 31, 2023.)

THE WORK THAT GIVES ME goose bumps is the process of transformation and change. I like coming in and assessing situations, doing my listening tour, seeing opportunities to improve a marketing program, and putting together a framework to get us to the next stage. The process is long, not necessarily because it's complex but because it involves change. I spend a lot of time evangelizing, demonstrating to people the ideas and practices we are implementing are founded on good, solid marketing fundamentals. I use industry research and analysis to bring people on board and share customer success stories.

The most important thing for people to understand is that we're not changing for the sake of changing or because I'm a new CMO and want to redo the website. We're coming to drive meaningful business change, to align what we're doing in the marketing organization to the company strategy, and the steps we have to take for that alignment to happen. My listening tour is critical to the process. Stop, start, continue is the first thing I do when I walk in the door. I send out a request to the entire organization asking what they wish the company would stop doing, start doing, and continue doing. I then schedule a series of one-on-ones to understand the context of their answers. I refuse to make decisions for the first 45 or even 60 days. Although people are usually eager to get things moving, I need the information to make good decisions before my listening is complete. Listening is critical to my work, and I have found the higher you are within a company, the farther you are from the work. You need to see the day-to-day challenges. Creating a continuous communication cycle is the only way to know what's happening in your organization. We use communication to build trust, demonstrating that we are listening and addressing concerns rather than being dismissive. Once we set this foundation, we do pulse surveys every six months to check in. They are anonymous, and people are encouraged to speak the truth of their reality.

Truly sustainable change is evolutionary, so we set up the transition in stages. I use specific business outcomes so we can look back in a few months and see how far we've come. That becomes a new baseline from which we can look ahead. We always celebrate our wins. We put in a rewards and recognition program called the You Rock Awards, which is peer-to-peer recognition. Every month, when we have our marketing all-hands meeting, nominations are made. We have some rules—you can't only nominate a person you work with daily; it has to be somebody from another group you're collaborating with who went above and beyond. It's been hugely successful. After a period of transformation, there is always some next mountain to climb from the foundation. I don't lose sleep worrying about that next mountain because we have an incredible team. I believe in them and trust we will figure out the next steps together because of all the changes and growth we've already accomplished.

Years ago, I went through a leadership development course at one of the companies I worked at. I was the only woman in a room of 40 employees. They taught us the last thing you want people to see is that you have feelings. They trained us not to be empathetic, and that business is just business. When I became a CMO, this lesson was ingrained in me. I wanted to know every part of the company and have an answer to every question. Fortunately, one of my team members sat me down and told me kindly that I was making everyone incredibly anxious. It was a pivotal moment for me. I realized I needed to unlearn those lessons. The more I lean into empathy in all my roles, the better my team does. People tend to see leadership as a step to more money, responsibility, and better titles. It's actually the opposite; as a leader, your job is to make your team ridiculously successful.

My advice to aspiring leaders is to trust your instincts and have empathy. You have to care about the people on your team to be successful. It might seem counterintuitive, but something pivotal for me and my journey has been to run toward the dumpster fire. At every company, some project has gone off the rails. Other people have tried to fix it, and no one wants to be attached to it because it has failed. That is an opportunity to become known in the organization as a problem solver without taking on much risk. You will learn more in that experience than anything else because learning comes from a place of discomfort. You will learn more from your failures than you will ever learn from your successes. Never stop trying new things, because that's where the breakthroughs are. When you face challenges, find support. I'm part of this CMO geek group called the CMO Huddles. We get together once a month and problem-solve together. I'm a member of CHIEF, and they put you into core groups that meet every six weeks over Zoom. Hearing other women tell their stories and learn how alike we are is incredible. Sitting in that space, sharing, and being vulnerable with people I've never met lifts me up. Most importantly, keep speaking up and keep taking up space. You are very, very important to the world.

55

Leadership Is the Killer App

Tim Sanders is the vice president of client strategy at Upwork, the world's leading platform for freelancers and contractors. He is also a prolific author, including the New York Times bestseller Love Is the Killer App: How to Win Business and Influence Friends.
(Highlights from our interview, recorded July 7, 2023.)

THE AVERAGE LEADER HAS THE mindset of wanting to acquire talent full-time, which is a heavy process that can take months and is high risk, low information, and can lead to friction because long-term hiring is a hard decision. At Upwork, we focus on demand and are increasingly fractional. I talk to leaders about shifting their mindset from full-time first to what I call scientific or smart hiring, where we focus on the work and less on acquisition. When I think about talent gaps, these dependencies stand between work vision and reality. I speak to organizations once they have a vision for a deliverable and guide them toward employing talent to make that possible upstream.

There are two schools of thought on how to move leaders to think in new ways; endowment and scaffolding. Jonah Berger wrote a fantastic book, *Catalyst*, in which he identifies key barriers to change, how to mitigate them, and how to help others take their foot off the parking brake rather than pushing it harder. Leaders are invested in the way that they do things. Simple things such as getting a leader off printing or file cabinets for financial management are harder than you think. Getting attorneys to move from FedEx to DocuSign has been a slog for corporations. It isn't because the old way is better; it's just familiar. We have a solid endowment to things we've been doing for a long time. My second thought, which is more contemporary, is around scaffolding and looks at how organizations protect the status quo at a structural level. This concept is from *Power and Prediction* by Professor A.J. Agrawal and his coauthors at the Rotman School of Management. The book, which focuses on AI, points out that many organization leaders will never use AI because they are so invested in rules generated by experts. They possess prediction and judgment power in the same body. Innovation is a leadership issue, not a technology issue. Successful AI deployment requires business leaders to be sponsors and catalysts, with technology leaders as the support system.

Not all leaders have the same goal; some work to enlighten people, to make them more powerful, more inspired, and give direction, and some are action-oriented leaders who are about building things whose focus is on outcomes. For thought leaders, the work is to fill in the information gaps with a sense of responsibility and diligence. You can't just pontificate; you need to research. I worked with Mark Cuban back in the '90s, and I've never met a person who was more of a voracious reader. When we met in '97, he had read at least 50 books cover to cover that year, about anything and everything. Reading informed him on a level I had never seen, and that knowledge made him the leader of our circle. Be unwilling to fall asleep on a business trip; take those four hours on your flight to Cleveland and read a book.

Leadership is a collaborative phenomenon. Anybody that says it's lonely at the top doesn't understand leadership because collaboration isn't the same as cooperation. Often, you talk to a leader who describes themselves as collaborative, but if you audit what they do in practice, at best, they are cooperative. Collaboration is when two or more people come together as equals around a shared vision. They share the risk, and they share the rewards. Collaboration only produces a stew of creativity when people feel equal to each other in working together. For leaders, true cross-functional collaboration is one of the best ways to solve complex problems and build an inclusive culture that creates the next generation of leaders.

Leaders know how to tell stories and understand which type of story is right for a particular situation. A story about you as a leader shares a sense of your personal experience that can set you apart in the room. When you and your team enter new territory together, a shared narrative is important because it moves credibility from you personally and unites the group. When dealing with a crisis, especially one that has happened previously in organizational history, the most powerful is the story of what we went through. Nancy Duarte's book *Resonate* and Joseph Campbell's work are essential reading for any leader looking to learn more about storytelling. Steve Wozniak, the cofounder of Apple, said that when you hear a story, it's almost like you've been induced into a hypnotic state, and the research agrees. When we listen to statistics, the wall of judgment goes up, but when you hear a story, you lean in and listen.

Not to go all Sheldon Cooper here, but I love to think about etymology. The word "work" was first used hundreds of years ago by a former French mathematician, physicist, and billiards enthusiast, Gaspard-Gustave de Coriolis. He was thinking about the work it took to move a billiard ball and used the phrase "good work" to describe a force that moves the ball toward the pocket. Organizations only produce value when they successfully deliver work to market. Whether that is a new product such as this book or a marketing program or customer support, the work must be delivered for value to be created. My focus is on how we can better increase both the velocity and quality of work, and the number one dependency is talent. No matter your work, it takes a lot of people to do the hard work of putting the ball in the pocket.

56

Executive Leadership

Debbie Owusu-Akyeeah is the executive director of the Canadian Centre for Gender and Sexual Diversity[1] (CCGSD), Canada's national 2SLGBTQIA+ youth organization. Established in 2005 because of the founder's challenges navigating homophobia within the Catholic school system, the organization aims to empower gender and sexually diverse communities through education, research, and advocacy. After 10 years, CCGSD rebranded to better focus on a national level of diverse communities who, over the years, asked for collective, national, or regional empowerment and education for their local leadership. This shift brought about a clear mandate and vision for the transformed organization to better educate, advocate, and empower communities sustainably. This was further cemented with Debbie's appointment as the new executive director in July 2020. Debbie is an activist, campaigner, policy analyst, athlete, activist, and earring maker who likes to bring fun into whatever she does, as she works toward ensuring we build a world that is better for everyone.

(Highlights from our interview, recorded September 21, 2023.)

I JOINED CCGSD AS THEIR executive director (ED) in July 2020, at the fresh age of 28 and at the height of a global pandemic. I was

---

[1]https://ccgsd-ccdgs.org.

committed to the organization's mission and where I, as a young queer person, wanted to see an organization like this go. A big part of that was to ensure we were weaving organizational change internally and reintroducing ourselves externally as a partner of choice in the national movement for 2SLGBTQIA+ rights. External reputation building was going to be important, but it could only happen with internal work to identify pain points and restructure the organization in a way that made sense to the young people we serve and employ, who are often working their first big-person job. Change is messy, change is difficult, but it is also beautiful. Over the past three years, there has been an ebb and flow, finding pain points and major wins in the organizational process.

I've always gravitated toward leadership roles but never in an individualistic way. I can probably attribute it to my upbringing, being the only girl in a family from Ghana. Growing up, there were very specific gender roles I was always pushing back against; I pushed back against things I didn't think were right, which has followed me in life. I was an athletic kid, but putting me into sports proactively wasn't a priority for my parents. So I took the initiative to fulfil my interest and played rugby in high school, provincially and then at the university level. My biggest lesson from sport is the ability to work as a team. Rugby has 15 positions, each playing a specific role, but some require collaboration with a different position. Rugby taught me project management before I even learned what project management was—that everybody has a role and responsibility. You practice your role. You go in and do your thing. You might have major wins, but those aren't necessarily the final score; they could be how many scrums you've won, lineouts, successful plays, et cetera. As a team and individual, you go back, learn, and readjust your plan accordingly.

As an ED, you're a problem solver, sometimes in more ways than you'd like to be. When I arrived, I spoke to everybody and did my own SWOT analysis (strengths, weaknesses, opportunities, and threats) internally and externally. I spoke to the board, ensuring they knew their roles and responsibilities and my own, created departments, and segmented the organization in a way that made sense and could foster collaboration across departments. An important part of change has been responding to what our staff sees from their perspective, listening, responding, consulting, and then making sure we're investing resources in the right way to build the organization collectively. When we don't have the answers inside the organization, we go out and find them, look at other organizations, and ask to share policy or procedural resources or bring in an external consultant to give a new lens to solve the problem.

My leadership has been shaped by intersectionality, a term coined by Kimberly Crenshaw. Intersectionality is an analytical framework that seeks to explain positional power; depending on the context, power can shift, contingent on norms ascribed to people based on their identities and systems of oppression that show up in the institutions we all navigate. From a positional power perspective, based on the systems of oppression or lack thereof, I might be in an oppressed position, where I could be vulnerable to the influence of someone who holds more power than me. In other cases, as ED, I might have the power to influence people. Intersectionality speaks in particular to the lived experiences of Black women in the United States but also to the challenges faced by many people impacted by systems of oppression. From a leadership perspective, especially in the context of a nonprofit, I often lean toward intersectionality to remind us in decision-making perspectives that those who live at the margins are the experts in their lived experiences.

In the context of CCGSD's work, one of its core values is participation; people benefiting from the services we deliver are coming along with us for the journey. As a youth-serving organization, we continuously incorporate youth advisory committees and create paid opportunities for young people to inform the projects we deliver. From a leadership perspective, we create opportunities for others to be as civically engaged as possible and participate directly in the communities that they live in. It's our responsibility to create the space for other voices to be heard. From an organizational perspective where there's relative power, that might mean allyship, co-conspiratorship, and creating resources, including funding young people to do things in their local communities. Leadership is connecting young people to the right folks so they can get their voices out there. It's hiring and paying them, treating them as members of your team so that they inform on a more institutional level what's happening within your organization structure.

I hear from young people that they are craving mentorship, specifically young 2SLGBTQIA+ people who, data shows, don't have as much access to mentors as their cisgender, heterosexual counterparts. Mentorship is where folks get to develop skills you don't get at school. Prior to becoming ED, I was working in roles many young people don't have the privilege of doing, like working at an international feminist NGO, working in public service, and being president of my graduate student association in grad school. Not everyone has those opportunities; mentorship, or even just sharing a few tricks and tips, becomes how information flows to people. It can be as simple as giving mentees access to your opinion on something like project planning, offering affirmation or support, or just sharing your story so others can see where you got to.

57

Leading through Innovation

Geoff Alexander is president and CEO of Wow Bao, a quick-serve, fast-casual Asian concept based in Chicago. He joined the parent company Lettuce Entertain You in 1993 and over the past 14 years, has grown the concept in different verticals, from consumer packaged goods, grocery stores, frozen, and fresh to dark or virtual restaurants in the United States and Canada, in airports, college campuses, and sports stadiums.

(Highlights from our interview, recorded June 2, 2023.)

A HUGE PART OF MY career has been spent leading through innovation. During transformation or uncertainty, leaders have to show confidence, vulnerability with an air of confidence. I am always looking ahead, paying attention to how things are changing. A leader's job is to think further and be in front of what could be coming during uncertainty. That doesn't mean, as leaders, we always have answers, but you have to come from a place of having your team's back. If I have your back, you'll have mine, and we'll get through uncertainty together.

Our brand lent itself to meeting people where they were, so we've focused on how customers interact with us and how technology can be better for our customers and employees. As early adopters, we anticipate the headaches new technology can bring. To make it work, you must first go to employees and explain why you're investing in something new. You need to be with them when the technology is deployed, because there will be challenges. Without information and support, employees won't buy into innovation, and it will fall apart. We look at technology to enhance customer experience and make the employee's job easier. As a leader, you must be willing to adjust ideas to your business. Everyone is moving at the speed of light, and the restaurant industry is trying to keep up. But technology in the restaurant space is never made by restaurant people, so we have to continually change our business to fit technology because it will never change to fit our business.

I take the word "partnership" to heart. A true partnership has to be on equal footing; it can't be transactional. Walking into a partnership, know what you need to get out of it, but also understand you will be giving. As we've grown, we've been fortunate to bring a lot to the table; we're going to get a lot of press and ensure your name is on everything we do. We're going to share the excitement, and we're going to be in the trenches together. Because if this thing launches and there's a mistake, I will call you up, and you need to take my call. I prefer to think of us being in the hospitality business instead of food service. We need to be giving hospitality to our consumers, our partnerships, and our employees. If you take care of your employees, your employees will take care of your guests. Everybody wants to be treated with respect. Everybody wants to know why. Everybody wants to believe in what's happening. Giving that hospitality, whether it's the extra day off or showing respect to everyone you speak to, translates on a more significant level.

At Lettuce, we have a steering committee comprising all divisions' heads. When I began my career, I wanted a seat at the table, and being invited was a huge accomplishment. As excited as I was, when I spoke, no one would listen. People would talk over me and have their conversations; it was incredibly frustrating. I knew anger wouldn't get me anywhere, so I worked on my communication. I took Own the Room, a three-day course in New York City. There were 400 people in attendance, with sessions on communicating effectively. On day one, I had to stand in front of everyone and present something, anything. It was terrifying. Who knows how I did? It didn't matter. The purpose was to gain confidence and learn to accept and use feedback, whether it was silence, praise, or an argument. When I learned to focus on my communication—that was when I stepped into leadership in a meaningful way.

The question is, as a leader, are you threatened, or are you challenged? Too many leaders feel threatened—by the competition, the economics of business, other leaders in the room, and their own teams. All of that puts you on the defense against those you should be collaborating with. Feeling threatened gets in the way of hiring the best people. As your business grows, you need to delegate—hire people you trust, and let them do their job. When I hire, I have a responsibility to help employees progress and ensure they feel challenged and engaged; otherwise, I've failed.

Successful leaders know it's not about them; it's about their team. We give staff opportunities to learn about different business areas, make sure marketing understands the supply chain, and bring home staff to work in the restaurants. Once a quarter, we have all-hands-on-deck meetings, where each department presents the previous quarter. We share successes, challenges, and lessons learned. If you're not educating your team, you're not motivating your team, and it starts with yourself. Keep learning and find new ways to connect and provide opportunities. Every day in our business, we do something called Do Teach Learn—every day, you have to do your job, teach something, and learn. That is how you grow a business. It starts with a hunger, and you have to keep people hungry. As a leader, you have to feed that hunger.

58

Thought UnLeadership

As a professional speaker, Scott knows a few things about sharing a message. From the time he was 12 years old, he wanted to be a speaker. Sitting in his living room, too lazy to stand up and get the remote to change the channel, he sat and watched a PBS fund drive as Les Brown took the stage. "That," he thought, "when I grow up, I want to be that." Since then, he's given hundreds of keynotes and spoken to audiences all over the world, had applause and a few heckles, seen too many airports and hotels, and once fell off a stage.

Even if you aren't a speaker, or don't aspire to take the stage with your ideas, being able to communicate in front of a group, your team, and those you wish to motivate is an important skill for leaders. Scott is incredibly comfortable on stage. He's missing whatever synapse it is in the brain that is supposed to make him nervous. He doesn't get butterflies, and it's not because he doesn't care, he simply feels, all the way through, that he belongs on stage. He's spoken around the world—in clothes he bought at the hotel gift shop (because he lost his suitcase) and sick as a dog (parasite picked up in Istanbul). He's only been nervous once, briefly before being inducted into the National Speaker Hall of Fame. That said, even for Scott for whom the stage is very comfortable, his speaking has changed and improved over time. Like any skill, practice and putting in reps is incredibly important. Public speaking is a craft that equals talent times experience, over time. Being good at it is one of the most powerful skills anyone can have in leadership. Too many brilliant ideas expressed badly have been passed over for terrible ones delivered with power. Being up on that stage is a privilege not to be taken lightly. Whether you're speaking to your team about a new project, your boss, your company, or your students, your words have the power to effect change.

When we think about leadership, we often think of those who use their voices, are courageous, and speak up. Leaders share their big ideas, which can be disruptive, and doing so can be risky. Even when changes are small, as humans we tend to resist changing our patterns and things we're used to. You might not be leading a big social movement or trying to right an injustice, but even implementing a small change is going to come with some risk, and using your voice can be intimidating. The leaders we spoke to who led transformations and change understood the potential risk and planned for impact. To do so, they built consensus around their ideas strategically, over time. The more people they brought on board, the lower their individual risk became.

During our interviews, several leaders recognized for their advocacy mentioned shine theory as a framework that has helped them build communities of support around their work. Shine theory is a term coined by Aminatou Sow and Ann Friedman, who wrote about the concept in their best-selling book *Big Friendship: How We Keep Each Other Close*. According to the authors, shine theory is "an investment, over the long term, in helping someone be their best self—and relying on their help in return. It is a conscious decision to bring your full self to your friendships, and to not let insecurity or envy ravage them. Shine theory is a commitment to asking, 'Would we be better as collaborators than as competitors?' The answer is almost always yes. People know you by the company you keep. Shine theory is recognizing that true confidence is infectious, and if someone is tearing you down or targeting you as competition, it's often because they are lacking in confidence or support themselves. It's a practice of cultivating a spirit of genuine happiness and excitement when your friends are doing well and being there for them when they aren't. Don't mistake this for networking. Shine theory is not about trying to help everyone you meet along the way in your career, because if you're doing it right, it's simply not possible to invest deeply in that many people. There are only so many hours and so many email replies in any given day. Shine theory is intentional. It is accountable. It is personal." (Shine Theory, n.d.)

How much of your work as a leader would be easier if you asked, "Would we be better as collaborators than as competitors?" When we focus on our goals and do the work to bring people on board, speaking out becomes more possible. Leadership isn't something you arrive at; it is something you embody in your every decision and interaction. Speaking up, speaking out, and sharing your vision is the bridge between your idea and action.

59

Leaders Intervene

Julie S. Lalonde, *is an internationally recognized women's rights advocate, public educator, speaker, and trainer with a focus on bystander intervention and community care. Her clients include the Canadian Armed Forces, Premier Justin Trudeau, and L'Oreal Paris. Her memoir* Resilience Is Futile: The Life and Death and Life of Julie S. Lalonde *won the 2020 Ontario Speaker's award and was named one of the best books of the year by CBC Books and the* Hill Times.*
(Highlights from our interview, recorded June 12, 2023.)

EVERY HUMAN BEING HAS A story, whether it's a really funny one they tell at a party or a traumatizing story that explains their core. There is something beautiful about the foundational concept that people are always learning and unlearning, that we can change our minds. I work in education because people do better when they know better. You have to create a path for people to redeem themselves. Communication is at the heart of my work. I am fascinated by how people communicate discomfort, whether they are being harmed or uncomfortable with the harm they are witnessing. The bulk of my work is teaching people how to communicate what they already know to be true. Something might be wrong, and you need it to stop. It could also be the elephant in the room that we need to name.

We unpack how people communicate their needs and other people's needs and how to do so in a way that has the desired impact. My advice is always to say something, and it's born from research that shows when one person intervenes, others are more likely to jump in. As the first person, you rarely share an idea not already held by others in the room. People talk about the bystander effect as a diffusion of responsibility. Still, another element is waiting for permission before getting involved, the seconds of courage it takes to say, "Hey, we all heard that, right? We all see what's going on here." Those two seconds of courage make a tremendous difference.

My father is a leader in IT, and my mother was an entrepreneur and a stand-up comedian, a professional clown, a children's entertainer, and an award-winning theatre actress. They taught me about storytelling and disarming people with jokes. My work is heavy, and when people show up, they are usually ready to be bummed out. Breaking that tension with humor is powerful and levels the playing field between me and my audience. The best compliment my work can get is for people to be honest and admit that they don't intervene because it's not worth it for them to stick out their neck for another person. Is that hard to hear? Absolutely. But it is also true, and I know they're telling me because I created space for honesty instead of just the "right" answers.

People don't connect emotionally to theory and statistics. Many assume if everyone knew the numbers—for example, one in three women are sexually assaulted—it would be enough. But people need to feel a personal connection to be compelled to act. When planning a keynote or training session, I think about taking people on a journey where I hook them right away. I'm a person who's going to be real with you, which means you can be real with me. It's a bit of a bait and switch; you think I will tell you a sad story, but I'm really sharing what you can do to fix it. I'm all about the Trojan horse; wait, you want a sad survivor story? I got that for you. And then, feminism!

Years ago, my father taught me something I bring into my work today: the orange problem. Let's say we were to go into a space, and I told you, "The solution for gender-based violence is orange." You agree, and we nod at one another. Orange is the solution. We set off, each on a mission for orange. The problem is one of us is looking for the color, the other the fruit, and both of us are convinced we're working toward the same goal. I share that story with audiences because I want them to ask questions. If they need to learn what an acronym means, I want them to ask. Most people want to be doing the right things, but they're intimidated to ask questions because, in our society, that denotes ignorance. That said, my work is not without tremendous risk. I've been the target of a national campaign with the Canadian Armed Forces coming for me and had the CBC warn me to leave the country before a story drops because they couldn't guarantee my safety, all of which was terrifying. I can't speak in public without a security protocol, even though I am privileged as a white Canadian traveling with a Canadian passport. Even with the backlash, I have no regrets.

My advice for others looking to get into this work is to take care of yourself and anticipate as much as possible. Don't come alone, have someone walk you to your car. The very nature of the work is that one day, someone may decide you're a villain, and you'll be targeted. Fall back on the people who remind you you didn't do anything wrong by speaking truth to power. Every two and a half days, a woman is murdered in Canada. I can't speak dispassionately about that. We live in a world where we all know stop, drop, and roll, but few of us have been on fire. We know learning CPR is important, even if we aren't a medic. I've gotten so many requests in Toronto because of attacks on the TTC [public transit] recently. If your employees are commuting to work, this is a concern they may bring into work with them, so why can't the workplace be part of the solution?

60

Demystifying Leadership and Innovation

Amber Mac is president of AmberMac Media, Inc., an award-winning content development agency, an award-winning podcaster (This Is Mining, The AI Effect), and a bestselling author. She is also the co-host of the weekly emerging technology radio show and podcast #TheFeed on SiriusXM. In 2022, Amber joined the board of directors at GFI (TSXV: PEAS), a plant-based farm-to-fork food and ingredients company. She is a regular business host and expert for Fast Company, CNN, Bloomberg, CBS, BNN, CTV, The Marilyn Denis Show, and SiriusXM. Amber specializes in creating content that helps demystify technology.
(Highlights from our interview, recorded June 12, 2023.)

I'VE BEEN SPEAKING ABOUT INNOVATION for 15 years, and whenever I do a keynote, someone asks me about the impact of technology on kids. Many are parents looking for answers and leadership because it feels as though things are moving too fast. It is hard to stay on top of the constant change, even for someone like myself who is immersed in the industry. About a year ago, I began tying together content around technology, the climate crisis, and bettering the world for the next generation—these values drive my work and should motivate all of us to have a clearer perspective as leaders.

Innovation can be an intimidating word; it often feels unattainable, requiring millions of dollars in investment and fundamental changes. Most businesses aren't innovating; they're adapting. Once, the technology sector was its own industry, but now, the arms and branches of technology reach out and impact every business on the planet. Leaders don't necessarily need to understand every detail of innovation—but they absolutely need to be able to relentlessly adapt to the future on our doorstep. Across industries, leaders have a responsibility to immerse themselves in the impact of technology and to understand both the threats and opportunities. This cannot be outsourced—the leaders of tomorrow will be those who understand the broad impact of technology and how to integrate it into their businesses well.

When we think about new technology like artificial intelligence and the future, it is natural to worry about where these developments will lead us. One of the most concerning elements is the number of big tech companies run by leaders who are only interested in one thing: profits. Many people will say, "Well, that's the role of businesses; they must be profitable," but technology affects people's lives. We are starting to recognize that we need leaders in the technology industry who are leading in a people-first way and who recognize the effects technology has on humans in the long run. We need bigger voices who understand that AI can be incredibly advantageous in our society but needs guardrails to ensure we put humans first. When I think about Canada, I see incredible opportunities to be a future leader in several important areas. This is true for AI research, critical minerals in the electrification of vehicles, clean technologies, human rights, and social justice. Many people don't realize that in the early 2000s, Canada was the first country to put warnings on cigarette packages and just recently announced warnings on individual cigarettes. If we can lead in this way to protect Canadians, we can be leaders in areas of technology regulation.

The most important leadership topic today is trust. To build trust, you need consistency and transparency. We know from research that there's a huge erosion of trust when it comes to certain types of institutions. To rebuild that trust, transparency is going to be critical. That doesn't mean you have to go out and share every moment of your personal life, but it certainly means that you make an effort to be transparent about relationships, partnerships, and your impact on society. To face the crisis we are in now, whether climate or technology, we need more consensus and community builders. We need different perspectives at the table. When it comes to leadership of the future, the biggest opportunity is within partnerships. Imagine the potential for a business leader to work with a competitor to create a partnership that would help reach more people and bring their communities together. Leaders must put their egos aside and focus on the potential partnership benefits to their businesses, customers, and clients. That's not a small thing. We have seen over decades that being a business leader can be an ego-driven role. If we start to see a change in leadership and more diversity and inclusion among leaders, we will create more successful businesses and a new generation of leaders with an ethical standpoint.

Communication is one of the most underrated leadership skills. In this age of misinformation, we desperately need transparency and truth communicated more by leaders. In what many call a "post-truth era," online spaces fill up with other voices when people don't speak truth. While I might prefer to wake up, put my head down, and go to work, that is not helpful in a world that needs strong voices on topics integral to the success of our society and the next generation. As most people embark on their careers, their aspirations are often squashed by the realities of working for their employer or clients or just limited by the world we're all in. We are often told to quiet our voices and play nice. However, aspirational leaders who use their voices for good and speak up on behalf of others are more successful leaders for more successful businesses. The media landscape has changed tremendously over the last two decades. I've always been excited about the potential of technology to allow everybody to have a voice and become what we now call content creators. At the same time, we've created this terrifying scenario where there's no editor among this large sea of creators. In real time, the landscape of journalism, researching, and reporting is changing. It's an exciting time for media leaders to step up and figure out how to impact the world positively. The reality of today's media is that every leader in business and beyond plays in the overall conversation; we're all part of the media.

Every day I've posted something others might consider "too political," my business has grown. I've started raising my voice, and my confidence has grown. I'm not talking just about views; I'm talking financially. Guy Kawasaki, a friend, told me years ago when he raised his voice against Trump, "Amber, for every person I lose, I get ten more." Most people are reasonable. They might be afraid to participate and don't speak up, but most people are looking for reasonable leadership. We've been told as a society to be safe, afraid to take a stand and use our voices, but we can't cower. I always wanted to get to this point where I could say what I meant and believed. It's so freeing and a privilege not everybody has. A woman earning minimum wage may not have a platform to support $10/day childcare, but I do—that is my responsibility as a leader.

61

UnLeadership Is Flexible

AFTER COLLEGE, SCOTT WORKED AS a national sales training manager for a packaging company, flying around North America teaching people how to sell bubble wrap. (Read that again. He literally sold air.) It was a sweet gig: two-day training, and 16 hours of talking about bubbles and popping packaging. His job was on the road, visiting customers and teaching them how to sell all their products better. It was actually great branding because they were helping customers have more business overall. Outside of trainings, he didn't do a heck of a lot. He went into the office and looked busy. He'd set the record for the quickest Costanza lap around the office with a clipboard, with his hair all disheveled. The company had several locations, so he figured no one really knew where he was.

When his son was about to be born, Scott was getting ready to take parental leave, something we have here in Canada. Getting ready for the time away made him really think about what he was doing at work. His job wasn't in the office. He realized he could keep working, travel on the weekend to save the company money, and do the rest of his work from home. He wasn't staying in expensive hotels, and his food expenses were pretty much Popeyes and Waffle

House. After parental leave, there was actually no reason for him to return to the office regularly at all. He decided to pitch it, put all the information together, and met with the company president.

"Come on in, Chris."

Well, not a great start. His name is fully Scott. But he sat down and kept going.

"Look, my son's about to be born, and I'm going to be taking four months off for parental leave."

"Can we stop you?"

"No."

Again, things were not going great. . .

"When I come back, I would like to work from home. I will still do all the traveling, but there's no reason for me to work from here. If I am not able to do that, I won't be coming back."

The president replied, "We are not ready for telecommuting [that's what it was called back then]. We'll just see you when you get back."

And that was the last time Scott worked at an office, 22 years ago. He loved doing the training and with flexibility would have stayed with the company. With the freedom to work from home, he would have been more productive, and the company wouldn't have lost the investment they'd made in hiring and training for the position already.

According to research, the best places to work (aka those with the highest retention) accept hybrid work is here to stay and are focusing on ways to make it work best (Agrawal 2023a). The hybrid model combines work in the office with work from outside the office (at home whether nearby or oceans away, on the road, etc.). Hybrid schedules can vary a lot between companies, teams, and roles, anything from several days per week of office work to the occasional stop in for a meeting. Sixty percent of employees with remote-capable jobs want to work in a hybrid work arrangement (Gallup 2023b).

With another 16% of workers wanting fully remote work, that means almost three-quarters of people are looking for flexibility and a change to the traditional Monday to Friday, nine-to-five routine.

For many, the introduction of hybrid work because of COVID revealed and highlighted problems with office culture. Several factors come into play, such as commute times and costs and the ability to take care of personal responsibilities such as child or elder care more easily. Workplace politics and discrimination can make the office an undesirable place to be, affecting mental health and overall success and happiness on the job and off. For example, for many Black employees, remote work lessened racism experienced at the workplace, with hybrid and remote arrangements increasing Black workers' feelings of belonging at work and boosting their ability to manage stress (Subramanian 2021).

It is challenging to embrace hybrid work because it fundamentally changes how employees and teams interact and experience being part of your organization. However, with only 20% of remote-capable employees currently working on site (down quite a lot from 60% in 2019), fully in-office work will be a relic of the past. According to McKinsey & Company, leaders should consider several factors when building an inclusive, hybrid environment (Dowling et al. 2022). These include work-life balance support; leadership that appreciates the demands, responsibilities, and interests of people outside of work; and improved and redesigned team-building processes that focus on belonging and fight against disengagement and division both inside and within teams. Furthermore, their data pointed to the importance of building mutual respect and open communication.

Flexibility in leadership means finding ways to connect and facilitate team building and understanding the needs and wants of your workforce. Rather than looking at hybrid work as a detriment, consider the ways it can improve your business and widen your talent pool geographically to find the most talented candidates and build the most effective teams. The future of work is flexible, and although many employers are concerned hybrid work leads to disengagement, data shows that remote and hybrid workers tend to have significantly higher employee engagement than on-site workers.

In the end, if you as a leader are mandating or encouraging a return to the office, it is your responsibility to make sure you give your teams a reason to be there and work to create a safe and supportive environment for everyone.

62

Leadership and Human Resources

"Failed HR lady" **Laurie Ruettimann** *has spent over two decades revolutionizing the world of work through her candid storytelling, innovative solutions, and passion for driving better employment experiences, dedicating her career to increasing employee retention rates and improving job satisfaction by challenging the status quo and empowering change. She is a respected consultant, keynote speaker, punk rock HR podcaster, and best-selling author of* Betting on You: How to Put Yourself First and (Finally) Take Control of Your Career. *Laurie is currently working on her second book,* Corporate Drinker, *about how to survive, thrive, and build culture in the boozy world of work and alcohol.*

(Highlights from our interview, recorded June 19, 2023.)

INDIVIDUALS AT EVERY LEVEL OF an organization should be self-leaders first and lean into individual accountability, no matter their job title. This means being the best version of yourself and modeling curiosity, empathy, and compassion, and connecting with your community, so when called up, you can inspire, coach, and help others become their own leaders. Leadership is helping others understand they are the CEO of their own lives; if they're making good decisions for themselves and their communities, they will have a positive effect up and down the organizational chain.

When an organization is doing its job well, nurturing people and allowing them to work at the intersection of purpose and meaning, they need little oversight from human resources. Rather, HR works to create a system with an infrastructure of technology, process, and coaching, and the work comes through managers, as the point of human contact. Leadership sees themselves as HR; and a light, nimble department is there to support and advise. However, when a leadership team doesn't like working with people, you end up with a complex HR department. Many business owners make the mistake of hiring, managing employee engagement, and coaching themselves, when they should be investing in HR consultants. Going to the marketplace is also an opportunity for leadership to learn so that if/when they choose to bring HR in-house, they understand what needs to be done. The idea that any successful business needs a big HR department is outdated; there are many ways to get leadership, hiring, and retention expertise into your organization in creative ways.

As a leader, it's easy to listen only to yourself, your clients, and bosses and forget about those who work with you. Many leaders mitigate this disconnection with a survey, as if a survey has ever saved a business. What is important is how you use survey data and the bravery of your workforce to speak truth to power. Good communication starts with relationships; a disconnected leader needs to take the time to get to know people they work with and express themselves with honesty and vulnerability. Leadership requires introspection, which is often ignored when driving deadlines and budgets. Often, leaders will tell me they'd be better if they had more time, so we begin with their calendar, by deciding what's important and necessary. If you have time for TikTok, to bemoan your competition while reading the *Wall Street Journal*, or go for lunch or coffee, you have time to ensure you're showing up for employees. A survey is a sign of failure; calendar management is one of the killer apps for good leadership.

Leadership is about curiosity and learning because when you're learning, you're growing and thriving, and that's the point of life. The world beats curiosity out of us, so if we retain any glimmer of it, we need to own that and fight for it. Curiosity saved me from working-class poverty. I became pregnant at 16 and realized I could succumb to fear and despair or fight for myself. Instead of taking a path of poverty and lack of education, I didn't go forward with the pregnancy. Instead, I became the first person in my family to go to college and live abroad, to have a corporate job, ascend the ranks, and become a consultant and author. I just kept marching forward, and that's part of being curious—the march toward something greater on your own terms. Learning saved my life. There are people in the HR and leadership worlds who think there's no place for this discussion in the world of work, but it has a tremendous impact. Many future leaders today are not afforded the choice I had. Not every person who accidentally gets pregnant is 16 years old; plenty of women in leadership positions will have less choice and have to go back and raise a child instead of starting a business or being the leader they wanted to be within their corporate framework. The implications are compounded by the fact that we have a maternal mortality crisis in America that particularly impacts African American women.

In the days of Aristotle and all those other old, white guys, they did an exercise called the premortem, where they'd figure out everything that could go wrong. For every point of failure, they would build a plan for success. In modern corporate America, Professor Gary Klein modeled a premortem for the modern world of work. Let's say you're part of a team building a new website. You look at how the last one failed—it wasn't accessible, the colors were wrong, you didn't plan for different programming languages, etc. For each point of failure, you brainstorm: throw out every idea, silly to serious, and give yourself time to plan around each of these ideas. According to Dr. Klein, your chance of success increases by over

30%. The premortem showcases blind spots and allows teams to fail in new and more interesting ways. I admire people who, after consideration, look around, listen, and watch and then decide to be brave. Once you make that decision, double down. This is your chance, and you don't always get a second one. We need more people in the world like you. When you feel something strongly, you are obligated to speak up. That is the burden of being a leader, and it can feel unfair, scary, and sometimes painful, but there isn't going to be a big sister who shows up to do the work for us. Take a swing, use critical thinking skills, and try. If you make an honest effort, you can't go wrong.

63

Leadership Sucks, and How to Fix It

Cali Ressler *has spent the past 20+ years re-imagining and revolutionizing the world of work, becoming an established global thought leader in the experiences humans must have in their organizations and with their leaders to sustainably perform at the highest levels to meet bold business goals. She is the co-author of two bestselling books on the future of work and evolution of leadership,* Why Work Sucks and How to Fix it: The Results-Only Revolution *and* Why Managing Sucks and How to Fix It: A Results-Only Guide to Taking Control of Work, Not People. *Cali has consulted with clients of all sizes across industries and takes pride in helping establish foundations for both people and businesses to thrive.*
(Highlights from our interview, recorded June 22, 2023.)

FOR AS LONG AS I can remember, we've been told, "People don't leave companies; they leave managers," but we never really believed it. Now, companies are having a wake-up call to the reality that's always been there; the landscape has completely changed.

It's no longer enough to say and do the right things to attract people to your company because if they arrive and the image doesn't match their experience, they leave. They don't give it a year or more; they're out. As a society, we are ready to be trusted—to live our lives, get the results we need to achieve at work, and be responsible for deciding how we will do that best.

When organizations move to be results focused, leadership is always surprised by how unclear their processes are and what people do at work. Traditionally, managers counted on watching things happen and seeing people working right in front of them. If I see Alison at work, I assume she's doing the right things. And if Alison works on the weekend or 60 hours a week, she is rewarded for that. But what if we focus on something other than physical presence? If we're results focused, we want to look at what Alison is achieving and how we measure that. This is the aha moment when leaders become wide-eyed and sit back—how will we know what people are achieving? Maybe we don't know what's going on in the company as much as we thought we did? This change requires a complete turnaround from managers, supervisors, and up. They have to change their perspective and can't lean on the things they used to do anymore.

Accountability is a big thing. If Alison and I have agreed she'll deliver by X date, at X quality, and that doesn't happen, we need to have a conversation, and something has to change. The answer can't be, "Alison, we need you back in the office." Instead, we have to talk about work and achievement. The conversation flips and becomes about performance on deliverables. This is a tougher conversation, and we tend to avoid tough conversations. It's much easier to ensure we see Alison on Monday, Wednesday, and Friday. Now we are talking about what we agreed upon, how that didn't come through as expected, why this happened, and how we can help support the work going forward. That is a genuinely empathic conversation, but traditionally, we saw this as conflict starting; it's a lot easier to say, "I want you back in the office."

I've worked with many companies and told their leaders they have to look at their business in a new way. That's challenging work. A lot of the time, you end up trying to work with insecurity that exists within that person. You're telling them they've misread their company's last 10, 20, 30 years or that they've avoided an issue. That insecurity shows up in a lot of different ways. I see announcement after announcement about calling workers back to the office, and my first thought is that the CEO doesn't think highly enough of their employees' abilities or wants to throw their power around because it makes them feel secure.

When I think about leadership, I think about communication. I'm a huge believer in followership, not in terms of following someone on social media, but do I see a person as someone I want to emulate? Communication needs to give people a feeling of "I want to follow that person." It's about authenticity and magnetism. When I see them, I know they're going to be the same person whether it's today, in a month, or in five years. They just are themselves, and that's really powerful. Many people try to become chameleons, playing games based on who they're speaking to, and it shows. People crave trust and autonomy and need leaders who show up consistently and authentically. For me, I'm a big music person. I have my kick-ass playlist of songs like Carrie Underwood's "Champion" and Sia's "Unstoppable." I share it with a lot of people, many of whom are stuffy corporate types, and sometimes it's just what they need. I know it's cliché, but we only have so much time to live a life. So if you're in a company that sucks and you feel like you have a kick-ass idea, go for it. Why would you not go for it?

64

Democratizing Leadership

SWAN SIT IS A BOARD director, creator, advisor, and investor. Raised before it was cool to be smart, she grew up to become the global head of Digital Marketing at Nike, Estée Lauder, and Revlon. She's now a creator with 3.7 million followers, with *Forbes* dubbing her the Queen of Clubhouse. A contemporary operator who sits at the intersection of corporate economics, digital transformation, and consumer attention, Swan is one of the most sought-after advisors and speakers in Web3. Sitting down to interview Swan was a joy; she seamlessly occupies the space between influencer and industry as a compelling storyteller and speaker.

When Alison spoke with Swan, she shared that democratizing information and access is her North Star. Swan's parents came to the States when she was six, from humble beginnings. Their dream was to send her and her brother to college. There was no Internet back then, so if you wanted to know anything, you went to the library. It was free, but there were still problems with access—you needed a library card and someone to take you to the library. Swan is all about access, about democratizing information. Talent is distributed evenly, but opportunity is not—how do we get more opportunity into the hands of more people? Democratizing information also means making it consumable. When you share an idea or build a brand, you're the explainer, the translator. Marketing a commodity with price, benefits, and features is one thing—but building loyalty requires emotional connection, creating a brand people can identify with that solves their problems.

Digital transformation is about technology but also people, processes, and culture. When Swan was with Estée Lauder, she and a group of others saw digital coming and knew it would change everything. They created a reverse mentoring program where each executive, head of a department or brand, had a millennial partner who lived on Facebook, Instagram, and YouTube. This was a way for them to ask questions and get hands-on experience, and it saved them from looking unsure in front of their peers or subordinates. Swan shared that it was the most game-changing thing they did to change leadership's aperture for digital innovation and transformation. Sharing knowledge shifted the culture and allowed them to build the processes afterward. It made everyone more open-minded and receptive to new ideas and created more authentic content.

The success of transformations are relationships, stakeholder support, and the shared vision. When Swan was at Elizabeth Arden, they were trying to grow the e-commerce business because that's how people were shopping. Here was the problem:

"The head of my Macy's account is bonused by the sales of Macy's in-person channel only; e-commerce is a threat to their personal livelihood, so they will fight what I'm trying to do. I can see this challenge coming. I need them to believe e-commerce increases our customer base, either the number of buyers or the frequency of purchases. One of the most important things we did was to make it one P&L, so it didn't matter if Macy's in-store or Macy's online for Elizabeth Arden grew. As long as the whole number grows, we all share in the bonus. What would bother me if I were the head of the

Macy's account? Probably a loss of control over the budget. So we developed processes where for an offline campaign, they would be at the head of the table, but we'd sit at the table. If it was a digital campaign, they would relinquish the control for us to have the driver's seat, but they would still be at the table. In one year, we put a full-court press on Elizabeth Arden selling on Macy's.com, which grew by 67% in one quarter. All of Macy's ended up growing."

People are predictable. You have to sit down with any transformation, consider the impact not just on the company but on each person, and create collaborative structures. Anticipating impact is one of the most essential skills to have in business.

According to Swan, in a corporate environment, people are often afraid of making big swings. If you're an entrepreneur, you might have seven failed companies before your eighth one survives. In corporate, if you make one mistake, you get fired. That's why people don't take big risks; it's not because they aren't creative and capable. The system doesn't reward it. One useful thing for big dreamers who want to take risks within a company is to learn to assess impact versus risk and lay that out for decision-makers. You can't only share your big idea and what could happen if it's a success—you have to understand what could go wrong and how to remedy that should it go off the rails. You need interim milestones to ensure you're on track, keeping checks and balances along the way. Big companies have more to lose, so you have to show risk mitigation and contingency planning.

In a more democratized business world, a democratized opportunity world, we have to change how we lead because it only serves one group and propagates one type of personality. Now, there are so many ways to win. The key is hiring people smarter than you, empowering them to do their best, managing in a way that brings out their potential, taking accountability, and serving that team. Swan is on the boards of two publicly traded companies, boards primarily made up of white men with an average age of 63. Now, she is not any of those things; if you want digitally native people on your board, you have to go outside those parameters. You can only lead if you listen to your employees and sell a product if you listen to your market. "Let's say, you're talking to white men, and they're resistant to diversification at Nike. It's a sports company in Oregon, very male dominated. But if you look at Nike customers, 60%–70% of the buying decisions are made by women, if not more now. I think the latest studies show about 85%, mostly moms making choices for their families. Serving women doesn't mean taking a men's shoe and 'pinking and shrinking it.' Women usually want the same cool men's shoe—just in their size—and a range of options for their family. We need to be more lateral in our thinking around the total addressable market, for different genders, races, and situations."

In Swan's work, she spends about half her time consuming content and learning and the other half curating for others. She shares her experiences, interviews others, and moderates panels—everybody, from Paris Hilton and Floyd Mayweather to Edward Snowden and William Shatner. She says, "I'm not necessarily looking for an aha moment but for the essence of humanity that makes people relatable." Her favorite question to ask at the end of an interview is always, "Fast-forward to the end of your life. What do you most want to be remembered for?" Her interviewee's answers are never a function of their achievements in business. "It's always about being a good parent or how they've helped people. I want to be remembered for helping make this world a little better place, whether it's democratizing opportunity and access or making people feel less alone and more connected. Without my corporate background, I wouldn't have the opportunities I have today; sometimes you need to go through journeys to get to where you find your purpose."

Swan's leadership vision leaves us with an important question: How do you want to be remembered?

65

UnLeadership and Crisis

EVERY PART OF YOUR BUSINESS is part of your brand: who and how you hire, your front line, the things you or your CEO likes on Facebook. Branding isn't in your hands, it belongs to your customers—it's what they think of when they hear your name and how they tell your story. Tech innovations have disrupted traditional relationships, how we hire, market, find our favorite foods, and learn about the world around us. They have changed the dynamic between brands and their markets, between students and their teachers.

To be in business today means one interaction at a local restaurant can change the face of a global brand. Customer service, once an exercise done one on one, now happens in public. The online world has blurred with real life, making them one and the same. Today, we learn the truth about unethical business practices with ease, while at the same time those seeking to deceive continually have new tools to do so. Now, before you go and throw your phone off a balcony, the good news is that in spite of innovation, good business is still good business. While news of your ethical practices, or lack thereof, may travel further and faster today, what makes them good has never changed. People do business with people they know, like, and trust.

In their 2022 book, *The Prepared Leader: Emerge from Any Crisis More Resilient Than Before*, Erika H. James, dean of the Wharton School of the University of Pennsylvania, and Lynn Perry Wooten, president of Simmons University, demonstrate that awareness is key to surviving and thriving through crisis. As two experts in crisis leadership, James and Wooten argue that the time to prepare for a crisis is always. Because human psychology is hardwired to avoid and downplay the impact of a crisis, they advise leaders to actively improve their awareness. In their framework, prepared leaders are sense-makers, who work to gather the perspectives of others from many possible angles. They work to have influence through transparency, building trust, and positioning themselves as someone who can shape other people's thoughts and actions. Prepared leaders delegate and facilitate leadership in others to create organizational agility and foster creativity toward problem solving and scenario building (James and Wooten 2022).

UnLeaders seek out and act on the advice of other people, and lots of them, whether experts, team members, or peers. Actively listening and seeking out knowledge keeps leaders from following their biases and creating bubbles or echo chambers. "Breaking out of the echo chamber and correcting for preconceptions isn't intuitive, nor is it easy. But it's essential in a crisis, because a crisis is hard to predict and understand in all of its dimensions. A crisis seldom plays by your established rulebook or existing structures. Unchecked, a crisis can evolve, expand, and engulf in ways we will struggle to imagine or anticipate. For this reason, when a crisis hits, you need your leadership to be as bias free, elastic, deft, and dynamic as the circumstances rapidly unfolding around you and your organization" (James 2022).

A leader often has to take risks just at the time when they least want to. Disruption creates uncertainty, and navigating it is at the heart of leadership. Whether it reveals leadership or grows it, facing the unknown is just part of the gig. Speaking with leaders, it's clear, when it hits the fan, leaders don't hide behind the fan, policy, or one of their employees; leaders face uncertainty and make others feel supported through the storm. For your business, the next crisis might be here now, or it might be around the corner, and preparation is the key. Consider your listening apparatus today: Do you have access to diverse voices and sources of information? Do you build your team members' ideas and feedback into decision-making? And how can you improve the listening systems and processes you have in place? Change is inevitable and challenges the status quo; UnLeaders anticipate challenges and plan for impact, which requires awareness and connection—with your team, with your industry, with your market.

66

Crisis Leadership

Dave Fleet is head of global digital crisis at Edelman, where he helps companies around the globe navigate digitally driven crises, dynamics, and channels
in order to safeguard their reputations. He has been featured in the NYT,
WSJ, Fast Company, Forbes, and more, talking about how companies can
navigate today's complex landscape.

(Highlights from our interview, recorded June 29, 2023.)

DIGITAL IS A THROUGH LINE for many big societal shifts we've faced
over the last few years, and that is only accelerating. This isn't an
optional perspective for communicators; people get their information online, and we have no choice but to think about that. Our
world is simultaneously getting larger and smaller, making leadership harder—we can connect to more people than ever before, but
our landscape is increasingly polarized. Bringing people together,
galvanizing them around a vision, and motivating them can be
harder when you work virtually. Effective leaders listen. They surround themselves with people who see things they don't.

Research is very much at the core of our firm. We've been doing
the Edelman Trust Barometer for 23 years. That's a huge study:
32,000 people in dozens of markets worldwide. The Edelman Trust

Institute oversees that study and constantly publishes new reports. We recently put one out around trust and brands and one around racial justice not long before that. Data-driven insights are always helpful but especially when there's a big gap between the perspective of the people you're talking to and the subject matter. The genesis of the Connected Crisis Study was reexamining how we look at the crisis landscape in general. We had a point of view on how things were changing and realized we needed to ground it in data. Through it we have gained an understanding of issues senior executives are facing and their perspectives, digging deeper into certain topics of interest. We use the report to start conversations with our clients about the risks they need to prepare for and offer ways to respond to different situations.

Stories are how we understand the world, but many organizations need to remember to think outside of what's important to them. They need to remember how their experience of the world might differ from those they're trying to communicate with. In crisis communications, you are typically dealing with emotional subject matter that speaks personally to people; the subjects have a material impact on people's lives. Communicating empathy through storytelling is critical, and organizations must remember that communication needs to be two-way. Even organizations that aren't household names, who don't get calls from the media about societal issues, need to answer to shareholders, customers, and employees about those issues. Many organizations get stuck in destructive internal conflict with differing opinions or values. We see inconsistency in decision-making and short-term decisions, where you focus on the problem in front of you but forget the ripple effects it might have. We help clients navigate their decision-making approach ahead of time so they can ground themselves when the rubber hits the road.

Decision-making approaches around engaging on societal issues vary by company but typically fall back on four consistent themes of consideration: company values, shareholder expectations, business impact, and credibility around the issue. The last is vital; companies need to ask themselves if they have credibility on an issue based on their past actions. You can't talk about diversity if your board is full of middle-aged, white dudes. Many of the organizations we work with land on this point—if you want to say things publicly, you need to make sure your own house is in order first. Consistency is critical because you need to have a consistent set of decision-making criteria to avoid finding employees and other stakeholders playing a game of gotcha with you. Building consistency builds trust. If you trust a brand, you'll give it the benefit of the doubt. Trust impacts all sorts of aspects of business. If your employees trust you, they will stay with you longer. They are going to be more willing to go above and beyond. When shareholders trust a business, the stock price goes up.

When customers trust a business, sales go up. It is built slowly and lost very quickly. Our view is that action builds trust first and foremost. Doing the right thing builds trust in the community. Our job is to help try and shape those actions and then help to communicate what's been done—do and then say.

My advice for aspiring leaders is to build resilience to uncertainty, and there are a few ways to do that within an organization. Make sure that the knowns are taken care of as best as you can. Make sure you are aware of what your risk landscape is, where your vulnerabilities are, and that you're working on these as best you can. Consider how you're paying attention and listening for signals that something might be coming. What's happening to others in the industry? What's happening from a societal issue standpoint? This is an area where a lot of organizations need to improve because they have gaps in their listening apparatus. Recognize you'll only be able to prepare to a point; other issues you'll have to deal with will make their way through. The key here is having systems and muscle memory to work through it and move quickly. You can only move quickly if you have done the hard work. No one wants to think about a crisis until they're in a crisis, but the ones who do are the ones who are better prepared for it.

When I started out, I thought leadership was about being the most important or loudest voice in the room. I've learned the opposite, that by definition, leadership requires you to leave yourself as the principal concept behind because it's about the collective. I don't have a single leader who has inspired me, and I don't like the idea of holding someone up on a shiny pedestal. I have many people I look to who I admire, and there are aspects of people's work I want to emulate. I surround myself with people smarter than me, who challenge me and keep me on my toes. The biggest mistake you can make in leadership is to assume everyone sees things the way you do.

67

A Note on Curiosity

IN ALL OF THE LEADERSHIP stories we've read, one of the common threads is curiosity.

Curiosity is about listening and seeking to understand. It is often stamped out quickly in the workplace, whether by overwhelming schedules or because it often leads to questioning the status quo. Leading a curious team is more challenging if you only have traditional tools. However, as we've seen throughout the book, curiosity drives awareness and engagement and allows us to find motivation and answers to challenging questions. Curiosity isn't about finding sources to confirm what you already believe to be true. Instead, it begins with awareness, accepting you may be wrong, unsure, or ignorant and then seeking to find a path forward.

One of the barriers to curiosity is an environment where you always have to be right and have all the answers. A leader who models imperfection allows opportunities for curiosity in their team. Curiosity also requires focus, so calendar management and finding ways to limit distractions are key. The leaders we spoke to are readers and audiobook listeners; they watch and listen to podcasts and spend time in conversation with peers, learning best practices. More importantly, beyond their personal habits and routines, these leaders facilitate curiosity at every level, in their teams and as an organizational value. Curiosity shouldn't be a privilege reserved for the top of the corporate ladder; as a company value, curiosity is transformative, facilitating innovation and a sense of belonging and meaning at every level of your business. When curiosity is encouraged, workers are less likely to fall prey to confirmation bias and stereotyping because they have better alternatives (Gino 2021). When we are curious, we view tough situations more creatively and are less likely to have defensive or aggressive reactions to challenges. Although it can be disruptive, curiosity leads to better results. UnLeaders understand that insubordination often leads to innovation. The fastest way to stop new ideas is to stick with the answer "Because that's the way we've always done it."

There are several ways leaders can facilitate curiosity in their teams: Be open to new ideas so that curiosity is rewarded instead of punished. Model imperfection and examine workflow and processes to ensure you are scheduling time for exploration and learning. Hire for curiosity and ask candidates about their interests outside of work; value applicants who ask questions during interviews and demonstrate their ability to offer new solutions and understandings. Model inquisitiveness by asking questions and listening to the answers; get to know your team, company vendors, and customers. Remember that curious people are listeners and approach challenges with creativity, not judgment. When we encourage curiosity, leaders become torchbearers sharing sparks that inspire further creativity and innovation and lighting the way through transformation and change. We have all been told curiosity carries risk (RIP, leader cats), but on the other side of those fears lie answers, answers we need to keep our companies and communities strong and moving forward. Leadership requires bravery, and so much of that begins with being fearlessly curious. You don't need anyone's permission to start; ask the first question and go from there.

68

Principled Leadership

Ty Francis is a Welsh American business development executive, entrepreneur, and corporate governance leader, with two decades of experience of business information management, data & analytics and evaluating ethics, culture, and values-based compliance programs. Ty is chief advisory officer at LRN Corporation, the global leader in ethics and compliance. He co-founded New York Welsh Inc, a Welsh diaspora business and social network, and JerseyForAll.org, a philanthropic initiative that empowers women, girls and people with mixed abilities in sports. Ty was appointed by Queen Elizabeth II as a Member of the Most Excellent Order of the British Empire (MBE) in 2017, and sits on the Business & Law School board of Southampton Solent University.
(Highlights from our interview, recorded May 30, 2023.)

WHEN YOU ASK EMPLOYEES ABOUT their company's values, many will be hard-pressed to tell you. Most executives will rattle off a mission statement, but true leaders will be honest and say they don't know or that they have done a culture survey and understand they have issues within the company. When you evaluate an organization's culture, you are really measuring how people feel and trying to understand the behavior of the entire employee base. It's something we do every day, and we ask questions such as, "Do you feel pressured to do your job? Do you feel safe at work, and does your organization understand psychological safety? Do you feel your company has a sense of organization justice?" We want to know if people feel they are equally and fairly treated. The answers boil down to a sense of the values that a company holds.

If you work in a company and feel valued, the company has probably done a good job of aligning its values with yours. It doesn't have to be an exact match, but they're going in the right direction and encouraging you to work hard and stay longer at the company. When the opposite happens, and answers represent a feeling of being undervalued, you create a transitory company where employees come and go. When people leave, they take their experience, intellectual capital, company and competitive secrets, morale, and inevitably, customer service suffers, and customers hate it. Companies lose a grip of who they are, and investors see profits dip. Hiring is hard, with increasing recruitment costs, time spent finding great employees, then more time onboarding those people. Imagine investing that amount of money and time in the people you have now; you create a dynamic and coherent environment. Sir Richard Branson is famous for saying, "Train people well enough so they can leave, but treat them well enough so they want to stay." It's not rocket science, but many leaders can be shortsighted.

Cultures that inspire principled performance take time to build, but once you have and maintain that culture, you outperform other companies across multiple aspects, including business performance, customer satisfaction, loyalty, innovation, and growth. In a recent study, we found companies that lead with values and value culture and ethics tend to outperform companies that do not, by about 40%. That's no joke. Ethical companies outperform their peers every time. Furthermore, beyond focusing on who you are as a company, you need to think about who you are, or are not, doing business with, how you are taking sanctions seriously, and communicating this to your employees.

The pandemic highlighted some companies' inability to understand where their employees were psychologically and mentally. Companies who got it and had leaders who stood up and recognized there would be a new way of doing things now are outperforming and outliving companies stuck in the past. Leadership has changed from having a job and a position that commands authority to leading with a moral sense of purpose and people following because of who you are and what you do, rather than what you say. The old adage, "Do as I say, not as I do," is changing. The spotlight on leadership isn't just from employees anymore; it's from customers, third parties, and investors. Things have changed, but many leaders are using the same apparatus in the same arsenal they did five years ago when the world moved on. The problem with institutional thinking at companies is that your average person is tied and tethered to that company culture because they can't leave. When a very famous bank was found to have cultivated a toxic culture (and was fined pretty heavily by the DOJ for that), people left but customers stayed, which seems to be contradictory to what I've just said. Here's the thing, most people aren't going to sell their house or change their mortgage when they see a social injustice at a faceless organization, so they tolerate the culture. But new customers will look elsewhere. But still, far too many companies thrive on workers tolerating toxicity. Employees are the lifeblood of a company; if they left tomorrow, those companies would crumble. Keeping those employees motivated is so valuable, and it boils down to your values and how you communicate them both inside and outside the company.

Traditionally, to demonstrate efforts to mitigate wrongdoing and unethical behavior, CEOs would present hotline numbers to a board of directors. Let's say they had 1,000 reports last month and 500 reports this month; most legacy thinking boards would assume that reporting has decreased and that things are getting better, but that data doesn't mean anything alone. If the number goes down, of course it could mean fewer complaints, but it could also mean people are afraid to report and more people are feeling pressured to stay silent. If the number goes up, is that bad, though? Have you made it easier to report, or could behavior be changing at your company? Then there are the complaints themselves. Those reports could be about someone eating someone else's sandwich or reporting about a terrible holiday party. But they could also be about how a manager was bullying them, how they've noticed a colleague is being sexually harassed, that we shouldn't be doing business in a certain country, or how we don't talk enough about LGBTQIA+ in the company. All of these reports are important. For a leader, it's critical to see reports as employee empowerment.

Whatever compliance or ethics program you have, it needs to be impactful, it needs to resonate with the employee, and that employee should feel engaged. When employees feel encouraged to speak up, your company does the right thing. Leaders embracing feedback and making changes will see the overall behavior of an organization change, not overnight, but it will change as an employee will see the result of their complaint or report actioned. They will feel seen.

It's also becoming harder for companies to shut their ears and say they don't get involved in politics anymore. Employees are looking at their leaders to lead by example and speak for them. The larger the company, the harder it is to weave in a tapestry of values because you have so many different people to satisfy. It comes back to facilitating open and clear communication. When a company puts out a statement supporting LGBTQIA+ people in a state where the governor says you can't say the word gay, that says something to employees about inclusion and belonging. It says the leadership cares about everyone in that company, not just a select few that align with a certain political belief. Now is the time. Leaders should be brave and bold and willing to stand side by side with their employees, organizations, and causes they care about. I admire sound moral decisions over sound business decisions.

Good companies are waiting in the weeds for employees who will come to work for them because of the values they nurture and create. Treating people well is the biggest competitive advantage in business. And it is not about having table tennis tables in your office or cool beer pumps in the office kitchen—it is a company's ability to make employees feel included, valued, and part of an organization that cares about them, their customers, suppliers, and communities. The investment community today is demanding companies disclose ESG (environmental, social, and corporate governance), human trafficking, diversity, water usage, and global impact on the environment. These aren't buzzwords anymore. Investors are making serious financial decisions based on those disclosures. This is no longer a nice thing to do; it is a must. It should be quite simple for any leader to see that the more ethical you are, the better business you're doing.

69

Leadership Goes Big *and* Goes Home

ONE OF THE HIGHLIGHTS OF our research on leadership was sitting down with adventurer, explorer, best-selling author, and faculty member at the Thayer Leadership Group at West Point **Alison Levine**. Growing up, maybe as a way to escape the oppressive summer heat in Phoenix, Arizona, Alison was drawn to stories of the early Arctic and Antarctic explorers and mountaineers. Although she was mesmerized by stories of adventure in really cold places, read books, and watched documentaries about people such as legendary explorer Reinhold Messner, who skied across Antarctica, she was born with a hole in her heart and Raynaud's disease, leaving her at extreme risk for frostbite. Alison never dreamed she'd go to those places herself; it was only after her second heart surgery, at 30, that a light bulb went on. She wanted to know what it was like to be out there. If those guys could do it, why couldn't she?

She went on to serve as team captain of the first American Women's Everest Expedition, climbed the highest peak on each continent, and skied to both the North and South Poles, a feat known as the Adventure Grand Slam, which only 20 people in the world have achieved. In January 2008, she made history as the first

American to complete a 600-mile traverse from west Antarctica to the South Pole following the route of Reinhold Messner, and again in 2016 when she completed two first ascents: Hall Peak in Antarctica and Khang Karpo in Nepal. In addition to tackling some of the most challenging outdoor environments, Alison also spent time climbing the corporate ladder, earned an MBA from Duke University, and spent three years working for Goldman Sachs. She left Goldman in 2003 to serve as deputy finance director for Arnold Schwarzenegger in his successful bid to become governor of California.

Speaking to Alison and reading about her accomplishments, it is hard to imagine ever being as brave. But Alison shared that she's never been able to leave fear behind. Instead, she embraces the mindset that you can be scared and courageous simultaneously. While most people love plans, Alison loves the unknown. "On a polar expedition," she shared, "you adapt to the environment, to what's going on around you and learn to pivot and shift." In 2002, when she led the first American Women's Everest Expedition, bad weather forced her team to turn around 270 feet from the summit. It was unexpected and out of their control, thwarting a mission they'd been working toward and dreaming of. As the leader, Alison was devastated. She internalized that failure, taking eight years to return to the mountain. When she did and made it to the summit—the big, critical moment—she realized something: "There I was, standing on a big pile of rocks and ice, and it hit me. The big moment hadn't changed the world. What was important was how I got there, got back down, and what I shared after the moment was over. Part of embracing the unknown is failure tolerance because if you're going to lead, you have to give yourself and your team the freedom to take risks and fail; you can't let failure define you."

In traditional leadership training, there is a lot of talk about overcoming fear and weaknesses, but there are some "weaknesses" we can't overcome, and we waste a lot of time and effort trying to.

Alison prepared as thoroughly as possible for her Antarctic expedition, training physically and meticulously studying the route and previous expeditions. Yet she was the team's slowest and weakest person during the expedition. At five feet four and 115 pounds, she couldn't keep up with those who were six feet four and 230 pounds and could drag 150 pounds of gear and supplies faster and more efficiently than she could. They were skiing 600 miles with a sled of all their gear and supplies harnessed to their waists; no amount of willpower, determination, or training would fix that. Another important part of their expedition, however, was protecting the camp. They shoveled snow into barricades around tents to protect them from the elements. While these six-foot-four guys were fast and strong, they had trouble with the short snow shovels for the barricades, wrenching their backs to bend and shovel. Do you know who was closer to the ground? Alison became the best damn snow shoveler on the team. That was how she could add value and contribute.

Another key lesson from Alison is that leadership takes practice, and leaders provide opportunities for others to take on the role. Every day in Antarctica, their leader, Eric, had a different team member out front leading the expedition, breaking trails, and navigating the route. The day he asked Alison was rough, and she told Eric she couldn't do it. In a whiteout in Antarctica, navigating is difficult because you can't see the ground or where the ground ends. Eric told her not to worry because he'd be right behind her, and he was, and she led. By the end of the trip, Alison was stronger because Eric had faith in her, gave her confidence, and was right behind her, offering support. Eric set Alison up for success, not failure. He wasn't waiting for her to make a mistake so he could scold her. He wanted Alison to lead, practice leadership, and let her know he was right there with her. You can tell your team members they're leaders, but it will only sink in once they've stepped into those shoes.

For Alison, leadership is also about legacy, about the positive impact she wants to make on the world. Rather than focusing on tenure, title, or having a certain number of people reporting to you, Alison teaches leaders to find opportunities to make an impact daily in all their relationships, interactions, and how they invest their energy. Currently, Alison is an executive producer of the documentary *Pasang: In the Shadow of Everest*. The film has been a passion project to share the story of an incredible and inspirational role model. Pasang Lhamu Sherpa was born in the Everest region and saw the men in her village climbing Mount Everest. She wanted to climb too, but the government of Nepal in the late 1980s and early 1990s would not let female Sherpas climb. At the time, Sherpa women were expected to stay home, cook, clean, and care for their families, and many didn't have the opportunity to go to school. Although she couldn't read, write, or speak the national language, Pasang Lhamu Sherpa dared to fight the government of Nepal for equal rights for all women in the country. After arguing that foreign women came to Nepal to climb a mountain in her backyard, she was finally granted access to the mountain. Sadly, she died in 1993 on her fourth attempt at the summit. Pasang Lhamu Sherpa was a freedom fighter who took on a battle for all women in Nepal. Alison believes we need courageous leaders to be brave architects of change. Alison hopes others will be inspired by Pasang Lhamu Sherpa's story to use their voices when they see injustice.

Perhaps the most powerful part of our conversation with Alison was how her views of leadership have shifted. "Hustle culture used to be so prominent, but we created a burnout culture. People on the trails who try to be the first ones back to camp often flop down in their tents afterward and can't function. You have to save something in the tank, and as a leader, you can model this for others and remind your team." Recruiting a team of the strongest climbers to tackle Everest only does Alison good if they care about team success. On the flip side, a team of cool people who all get along will only succeed if they have the needed skills. As a leader, you want to find a mix of skill, experience, and good team players.

"I used to be a 'Go big or go home' person, but now my mantra is, 'Go big *and* go home.'" Over the years, Alison has seen too many people go big and not go home, not because they were reckless but because they were in unpredictable environments, in the mountains or on a polar expedition with uncontrollable factors. Unfortunately, sometimes even the most cautious, experienced people can have a tragedy happen. And so, she has changed her thinking and wants to spread this mindset as much as possible to leaders. "We want our teams to have big dreams, stretch themselves, and get out of their comfort zones, but at the end of the day, the only thing that matters is coming home to the people you care about and who care about you. The people who get to the top of the mountain aren't necessarily the ones who are the most skilled or fastest; they are the ones who keep putting one foot in front of the other. That's how you achieve anything big—one step at a time."

70

What We UnLearned

We hope you enjoyed reading *UnLeadership*! We've had a lot of fun writing it and speaking about leadership with so many incredible people. Of course, there are many leaders who have inspired and guided us who are not included in this book and beyond that, countless more outside our knowledge or vision. *UnLeadership* is a collection of stories that make up what leadership means to us today, and we encourage you to find your own. The leaders we interviewed all shared the traits of curiosity, humility, and empathy; a desire, driven by values, to move others toward a better human experience. For every leader we've spoken to and learned from, there were countless others who inspired and shaped their journey: parents and teachers, pioneers, authors and researchers, bosses and coworkers, partners, and others who collaborated, challenged, and shaped how each saw and experienced the world of work.

UnLeadership is about vision, seeing something—a big idea, a framework, a solution—and leaning into that vision with curiosity. UnLeadership is about communication—taking that vision, and sharing it with others in a way that makes it seem possible and doable, that brings others onboard as collaborators. UnLeadership is about accountability, not reward; it is about being in service to others. Often the most impactful leaders aren't CEOs or even managers—they're coworkers who welcome you on your first day, those who take time to educate, celebrate, and elevate others, bosses who see subordination as innovation, and coworkers who create resources and share opportunities. You can lead from anywhere—and in fact, you should. In the age of disruption, we need leaders at every level, in every industry, working to solve the complex challenges before us.

Leadership isn't a title—it is something you embody with every decision and interaction. It happens one play at a time, driven by values and impact. Awareness and curiosity make leadership a verb, a creative process. Self-awareness is the start—knowing that you bring your past experiences and emotions to work daily, whether you recognize that or not. Awareness is about power—understanding that, as the boss, you have no idea what it's like to work for you. Leadership is also about organizational and industry awareness. Leaders are curious, see gaps, and do the work of research and asking questions. Leadership is about gathering stories; a leader needs knowledge to have full thought. Leadership is a group project and requires decentering yourself, listening, and taking feedback. Avoiding conflict is avoiding leadership. Collaboration is greater than cooperation.

Successful leaders have empathy and humility. They understand they walk a path others have walked and need the knowledge/experience of others to take ideas and create action. Leaders understand relationships aren't transactional. They build community. Trust is their currency; they work on building it, nurturing it, and understanding it isn't a renewable resource.

Leadership is a relational skill; there isn't one ideal pathway to leadership or singular leadership style. Leaders share their values, vision, and goals. Through awareness and connection, leaders focus on communication and sharing their big ideas. Their ability to make their vision clear is paramount, as is their ability to translate this vision to others, have it stick, and travel. Leaders make everyone on their team the hero of the story.

Leadership is about helping others navigate transformations. Leaders often make rough waters feel smooth based on trust and their ability to share appropriate vulnerability, provide transparency, and keep everyone working toward a shared vision. Leadership requires risk and crisis management. Big ideas challenge the status quo. Anticipating challenges and planning for impact is the work of leadership. This requires awareness and connection—with your team, industry, and market.

Recently, on TikTok, we watched an interview done by Lewis Howes with the incredible Brené Brown. In the interview, Brené shared that she was shocked to learn in her research that the opposite of belonging is fitting in. "Fitting in is assessing a group of people, and thinking, 'Who do I need to be? What do I need to say? What do I need to wear? How do I need to act?' and then changing who you are. True belonging never asks us to change who we are; it demands that we be who we are. If we fit in because of how we have changed ourselves, that's not belonging because you have betrayed yourself for other people. And that is not something sustainable." Leaders create space for belonging—on teams, companies, organizations, and movements. They recognize each individual's value and collaborate because it builds trust and loyalty and moves the work forward.

When you look for examples of leadership, remember the most impactful leaders are often the quietest in the room and can go unnoticed and uncelebrated. Open your eyes, be humble, celebrate, and raise up those voices. Focus on self-awareness and lean into your curiosity. Do your research, build relationships, share your vision, and listen. Then listen some more. Root yourself in values authentically, do before you say, and then go for it—the world needs more thoughtful leaders like you. There is no one path to leadership—find others who inspire you, learn from them, and then become a leader others can look up to.

A Final Note

WE'D REALLY LOVE TO HEAR your leadership stories! What does leadership mean to you? Who are the leaders who've inspired your journey? What lessons do you have to share with aspiring leaders? How do you see leadership today and in the future? Send us an email to info@unmarketing.com and visit UnLeadershipBook.com. We'd love to hear from you!

Thank you to all the leaders in our lives, especially the most important ones, Aidan, Owen, Jakob, Alex, and Tessa. In everything we do, you're always the why. Also, a special thank-you to all of the leaders who so generously shared their expertise and time for *UnLeadership*. We encourage you all to learn more about their work.

References

Abrams, K., A. Phelps, K. Lu, and V. Firth. 2021. "The Health-Savvy CEO." *Deloitte Insights*. https://www2.deloitte.com/us/en/insights/topics/leadership/ceo-role-employee-health-wellness.html.

Agrawal, Sangeeta, and Ben Wigert. 2022. "Returning to the Office: The Current, Preferred and Future State of Remote Work." Gallup.com. https://www.gallup.com/workplace/397751/returning-office-current-preferred-future-state-remote-work.aspx.

Annie E. Casey Foundation, The. 2023. (March 13). "What Are the Core Characteristics of Generation Z?" https://www.aecf.org/blog/what-are-the-core-characteristics-of-generation-z.

Asana. 2022. "Burnout Statistics You Should Know to Keep Employees Engaged." https://resources.asana.com/americas-anatomy-of-work-burnout-ebook.html.

Change Enthusiasm. 2022. "2022 National Study: Change and Emotion in the Workplace." https://changeenthusiasmglobal.com/wp-content/uploads/2023/02/Change-Enthusiasm-Global-2022-Whitepaper.pdf.

Dowling, B., D. Goldstein, M. Park, and H. Price. 2022. "Hybrid Work: Making It Fit with Your Diversity, Equity, and Inclusion Strategy." McKinsey & Company. https://www.mckinsey.com/capabilities/people-and-organizational-performance/our-insights/hybrid-work-making-it-fit-with-your-diversity-equity-and-inclusion-strategy.

Future Forum. 2023. "Future Forum Pulse." https://futureforum.com/research/future-forum-pulse-winter-2022-2023-snapshot/.

Gallup. 2023a. "How to Improve Employee Engagement in the Workplace." Gallup.com. https://www.gallup.com/workplace/285674/improve-employee-engagement-workplace.aspx.

Gallup. 2023b. "State of the Global Workplace Report." Gallup.com. https://www.gallup.com/workplace/349484/state-of-the-global-workplace.aspx.

Goleman, D. (1998). "What Makes a Leader?" *PubMed* 76, no. 6, 93–102. https://pubmed.ncbi.nlm.nih.gov/10187249.

Graham, J. R., C.R. Harvey, J. Grennan, and S. Rajgopal. 2016. "Corporate Culture: Evidence from the Field." *Social Science Research Network*. https://doi.org/10.2139/ssrn.2805602.

Gino, F. 2021. (July 8). "The Business Case for Curiosity." *Harvard Business Review*. https://hbr.org/2018/09/the-business-case-for-curiosity.

Hatfield, S., J. Fisher, and P.H. Silverglate. 2022. "The C-Suite's Role in Well-being." *Deloitte Insights*. https://www2.deloitte.com/us/en/insights/topics/leadership/employee-wellness-in-the-corporate-workplace.html.

James, E. 2022. (September 13). "In a Crisis, Great Leaders Prioritize Listening." *Harvard Business Review*. https://hbr.org/2022/09/in-a-crisis-great-leaders-prioritize-listening.

James, E.H., and L.P. Wooten. 2022. *The Prepared Leader: Emerge from Any Crisis More Resilient Than Before*. Philadelphia, Pennsylvania: Wharton School Press.

Khan, S. 2021. (March 23). "When Work Feels like Family, Employees Keep Quiet about Wrongdoing." *Harvard Business Review*. https://hbr.org/2020/12/when-work-feels-like-family-employees-keep-quiet-about-wrongdoing.

Lancefield, D. 2021. (August 27). "4 Actions Transformational Leaders Take." *Harvard Business Review*. https://hbr.org/2021/05/4-actions-transformational-leaders-take.

Luna, J. A. 2021. (November 10). "The toxic effects of branding your workplace a 'Family.'" *Harvard Business Review*. https://hbr.org/2021/10/the-toxic-effects-of-branding-your-workplace-a-family.

Mayo Clinic. 2021. (June 5). "Job Burnout: How to Spot It and Take Action," Mayo Clinic. https://www.mayoclinic.org/healthy-lifestyle/adult-health/in-depth/burnout/art-20046642.

McKinsey & Company. 2015. "Changing Change Management." https://www.mckinsey.com/featured-insights/leadership/changing-change-management.

McKinsey & Company. 2022. (July 13). "The Great Attrition Is Making Hiring Harder. Are You Searching the Right Talent Pools?" McKinsey & Company. https://www.mckinsey.com/capabilities/people-and-organizational-performance/our-insights/the-great-attrition-is-making-hiring-harder-are-you-searching-the-right-talent-pools.

McKinsey & Company. 2023. (June 20). "Mind the Gap: Are Gen Z CEOs a thing already?" Mind the Gap Newsletter. https://www.mckinsey.com/~/media/mckinsey/email/genz/2023/06/2023-06-20b.html.

Robinson, B. 2023. (June 8). "3 Ways Gen Z Leaders Are Reviving The Revolutionary Energy Of The Sixties." *Forbes.* https://www.forbes.com/sites/bryanrobinson/2023/06/08/3-ways-gen-z-leaders-are-reviving-the-revolutionary-energy-of-the-sixties/?sh=44cffd69330c.

Sanchez, P. 2021. (August 31). "The Secret to Leading Organizational Change Is Empathy." *Harvard Business Review.* https://hbr.org/2018/12/the-secret-to-leading-organizational-change-is-empathy.

Slack. 2023. "The State of Work in 2023." Slack. https://slack.com/blog/news/state-of-work-2023.

Subramanian, S. 2021. A new era of workplace inclusion: moving from retrofit to redesign. *Future Forum.* https://futureforum.com/2021/03/11/dismantling-the-office-moving-from-retrofit-to-redesign/.

Udemy. 2018. "Udemy In Depth: 2018 Employee Experience Report." https://research.udemy.com/research_report/udemy-in-depth-2018-employee-experience-report/.

What is Shine Theory? — Shine Theory. (n.d.). Shine Theory. https://www.shinetheory.com/what-is-shine-theory.

"Work Happiness Survey." 2021. Indeed.com. Retrieved August 30, 2023, from https://www.indeed.com/career-advice/career-development/work-happiness-survey.

Index